Secret Subversion I

Mou Zongsan (1909–1995), one of the representatives of Modern Confucianism, belongs to the most important Chinese philosophers of the twentieth century. From a more traditional Confucian perspective, this book makes a critical analysis of Mou's "moral metaphysics," mainly his thoughts about Confucian ethos.

The author observes that Mou simplifies Confucian ethos rooted in various and specific environments, making them equal to modern ethics, which is a subversion of the ethical order of life advocated by traditional Confucianism. The author believes, also, that Mou has twisted Confucian ethos systematically by introducing Kant's concept of autonomy into the interpretation of Confucian thoughts.

Scholars and students in Chinese philosophy, especially those in Confucian studies, will be attracted by this book. Also, it will appeal to readers interested in comparative philosophy.

Tang Wenming is a professor in the Department of Philosophy and Deputy Director of the Institute for Ethics and Religions Studies at Tsinghua University. He is also Secretary General of the Chinese Confucian Academy. His research areas are ethics, Chinese philosophy and religious studies.

Routledge Studies in Contemporary Chinese Philosophy

It is widely recognized that in science, industry, and technology China is a modern superpower. However, there is still a common stereotype that Chinese philosophy consists of nothing but the earnest repetition of quaint sayings from long-dead sages. In actuality, philosophy in China today is vibrant and intellectually diverse.

The aim of this series is to publish translations of the best and most representative works by contemporary Chinese philosophers. The books in this series include contemporary studies of the history of Chinese or Western philosophy, as well as original works of research in ethics, political philosophy, metaphysics, and other areas. Routledge Studies in Contemporary Chinese Philosophy seeks to fill the large gap that currently exists in the study of Chinese philosophy by providing high-quality translations to English-language scholars.

Series Editor:

Bryan W. Van Norden, Vassar College, USA
Yong Li, Wuhan University, China

Titles in this series currently include:

Secret Subversion I
Mou Zongsan, Kant, and Early Confucianism
TANG Wenming

Secret Subversion II
Mou Zongsan, Kant, and Original Confucianism
TANG Wenming

A History of Classical Chinese Thought
LI Zehou, translated by Andrew Lambert

For more information, please visit: www.routledge.com/Routledge-Studies-in-Contemporary-Chinese-Philosophy/book-series/RSCCP

Secret Subversion I

Mou Zongsan, Kant, and
Early Confucianism

Tang Wenming

Routledge
Taylor & Francis Group

LONDON AND NEW YORK

This book is published with financial support from China Book International

First published 2021 by Routledge

2 Park Square, Milton Park, Abingdon, Oxon OX14 4RN
605 Third Avenue, New York, NY 10017

Routledge is an imprint of the Taylor & Francis Group, an informa business

First issued in paperback 2022

Publisher's Note

The publisher has gone to great lengths to ensure the quality of this reprint but points out that some imperfections in the original copies may be apparent.

English Version by permission of SDX Joint Publishing Company.

British Library Cataloguing-in-Publication Data
A catalogue record for this book is available from the British Library

Library of Congress Cataloging-in-Publication Data
A catalog record has been requested for this book

ISBN: 978-0-815-37442-8 (hbk)
ISBN: 978-1-03-233600-8 (pbk)
DOI: 10.4324/9781351242257

Typeset in Times New Roman
by Newgen Publishing UK

Contents

Part I
The reduction of morality

Abstract: Part I criticizes the reduction of Confucianism caused by understanding the core of Confucianism in terms of Kantian modern moral concepts, led by Mou Zongsan.

1 Autonomy and altruism

On the moralistic interpretation of Confucian thought

Since modern times, the essential feature of Confucianism seems to be depicted by the term "moralism." Both thinkers openly bowing to Confucian thought and researchers with a critical approach to Confucianism seem to share an epistemological belief, i.e., identifying morality as a remarkable feature of Confucianism. This viewpoint not only can be confirmed with modern scholars of Neo-Confucianism, such as Xiong Shili, Liang Shuming, Tang Junyi, Mou Zongsan and Xu Fuguan, but is also acknowledged by most researchers who hold critical views of Confucianism. For example, a viewpoint that probably originated from Jesuit missionaries maintains that Confucianism is either ethics or moral philosophy, and the core of this viewpoint is that the fundamental aim of Confucianism lies in morality.

Then, how to accurately understand the connotation of moralism? Because of the polysemic nature of the word "morality," we first need to clarify the cultural and essential content carried and conveyed in the modern sense of "morality." From a structural point of view, the fundamental feature of morality is nothing but a rational autonomy, especially compared with obedience-oriented religious belief. However, what we need to explain is, such a viewpoint is a purely modern idea started by Kant. In Chinese classical literature, *dao* (道) and *de* (德) are fundamental and originary notions, while *dao* and *de* connected and used as *daode* (道德, "morality") is a relatively late notion. The use of *daode* by modern Chinese academia can be traced back to two long-standing conceptions in Chinese classical literature: *dao* and *de* were used in combination by Japanese scholars to translate "morality" from Western languages. From an etymological point of view, "morality" has an affinity with the Latin word *mores* (custom). In the Western ancient theoretical discourse, the foundation of morality was often attributed to nature or God, or the combination of both. For example, Aristotle maintained that natural teleology is the basis of ethics, while in the Judeo-Christian tradition moral commandments are given by God. We also know that with the development of Christian theology, theodicy has formed on the premises of natural teleology, which is especially evident concerning ethical issues, for example the relationship between the theological virtues rooted in God (faith, hope and charity) and the natural virtues rooted in nature (wisdom, courage, temperance and justice) discussed by Thomas Aquinas.

In the Age of Enlightenment, Immanuel Kant advocated the authority of reason within the moral issue, and he explained morality as a natural matter of practical reason, by adopting the concept of autonomy proposed by Rousseau in the field of political philosophy, thus relating the foundation of morality from nature or from God to reason. According to Kant's view, morality has to be considered as an independent and self-sufficient value. Since goodwill is a thing-in-itself, to act out of goodwill epitomizes the highest good, and best exemplifies the moral value. In order to defend the purity of moral value, Kant employed a rigorous formalistic argumentation, but it does not mean that Kant's moral concept lacks substantial connotation. If autonomy is considered as the formal standard of moral value, then altruism should be the substantial standard of moral value. Whether we resort to moral emotion or goodwill, or whether we adopt deontology or consequentialism, altruism is in fact one of the core meanings of modern morality. In this regard, Nietzsche claimed that, according to the prevailing practice of modern morality, "the essential characteristic of moral conduct is selflessness, self-sacrifice, sympathy or compassion."[1] The altruistic tendency of morality can sometimes be reflected by the universality appeal of moral views; it could be the universality of righteousness and sense of justice or even the universality of utility: the altruistic tendency is always a substantial element of moral value. In other words, an opinion will not be credited as directly connected to moral value if it does not consciously or unconsciously contain this altruistic tendency. Morality is always related to the altruistic tendency, which claimed to be self-oriented and refuses to be based on anything else, regardless of any theoretical forms. By connecting the formal standard and the substantial standard, we can then summarize the Kantian statement on the modern notion of morality as a pure and voluntary altruistic tendency.

Confucianism's explanation of moralism has prevailed since modern times. In general, given such a moralistic explanation, the ethical spirit carried by Confucianism is then described as a pure and voluntary altruistic tendency. Separately speaking, moralism is interpreted to understand the Confucian ethical spirit as a formal autonomy and essential altruism. As for the autonomy, when discussing Confucianism, the substitution of religion with morality, Liang Shuming advocated that:

> morality is a matter of reason and relies on *self-aware autonomy*. Religion is a matter of belief and lies in believers' obedience to precepts. Influenced by this opinion, China has been replacing religion with morality since Confucius. This is exactly the opposite of the nature of religion, that is, placing one's trust in others instead of oneself, and relying on others rather than claiming self-sufficiency.[2]

The main reason for Xu Fuguan to regard the concern-consciousness as moral conscience is that "the concern-consciousness is a manifestation of the human mind beginning to bear direct responsibility for what has happened, i.e., humans start to have self-conscious thoughts."[3] Besides, in Mou Zongsan's system of thought focused on "moral metaphysics," Kant's autonomy has great importance, and we are also very familiar with Mou's view. As for altruism, although Confucius claimed that "people in old times learned to improve themselves, but people at present learn to please others," both Confucius' "benevolence" and Mencius' "sense of compassion," and his theory of the goodness of human nature, are always reductively interpreted as a pure and voluntary altruistic tendency. Based on this premise, *wei ji zhi xue* (为己之学, "learning for oneself") is understood as morally pure and voluntary, i.e., a person actively and voluntarily does things for others. Here we can explain the willingness of a person according to the principle of autonomy. Moreover, since this moral ego is essentially, actively and voluntarily oriented to others, this altruistic feature can be recognized as its true nature. Similarly, in this context, Mencius said that "The principle of what is right and the sense of justice are agreeable to my mind, as the flesh of grass- and grain-fed animals is agreeable to my mouth." The "principle of what is right" and the "sense of justice" are radically regarded as a pure and voluntary altruistic tendency, and "my own heart-mind" is pleased when putting those principles into practice. I am willing to do things for others, or as Schiller said, I have "love for moral obligation."

In the recent theoretical tradition of Neo-Confucianism, Mou Zongsan's "moral metaphysics" is the highest achievement related to the moralistic interpretation of Confucianism. Conscience is seen as an innate moral emotion or goodwill, i.e., a transcendental moral substance. At the same time, it is a transcendental moral subject, namely the pure highest good as noumenal essence. Here "goodness" can only be explained in a moral sense, i.e., "goodness for others" rather than "what is good for oneself" beyond moral sense. Although some scholars used all kinds of reasons to oppose Mou's "moral metaphysics," none of them objected to the interpretation of Confucianism according to the category of moralism, especially in terms of its substantial spiritual aim. It seems that a wide consensus has been reached in academia, resulting in a self-explanatory common view that needs no further discussion. After all, who would object to the concept of "goodness"? We can say with certainty that the moralistic interpretation of Confucianism, through its current absolute position, dictates our intellectual and spiritual world. However, we must realize that moralism is sometimes mistakenly understood. For example, Nietzsche questioned this partial view on modern moralism using his genealogical method: is the current morality a sign of "the weariness, the distress, and the decline of life," or is it "an indication of the energy, the power, and the will of life, revealing the courage, the certainty, and the future of life?"[4] In his view, the moral understanding of ego undoubtedly lies on the premise of nihilism, and it includes depreciation of man's noble quality. It claims the absolutely worthless value of the ego and life, and even belittles humans to the level of animals. Therefore, for individuals, moralism is a sign of a decadent life, and insane striving for morality is merely used to conceal the poverty of life. For a nation, moralism causes cultural septicemia that will destroy the national spirit; thus, it does not deserve to be and is unlikely to be a nation's cultural life. If we consider Nietzsche's critical rational standpoint towards modern moralism, we should recognize that it poses a challenge to the unquestioned and widely accepted interpretation of the moralistic tendency of Confucianism. For those who support a moralistic understanding of Confucianism, the central problem lies in the fact that, on the one hand, they cannot consider or are not willing to admit the misuse of the moralistic tendency and, on the other hand, they lack a necessary reflection on the reductive trend to conceive of moralism as the fundamental spiritual aim of Confucianism.

Notes

1 Friedrich Nietzsche, *The Gay Science*, trans. by Walter Kaufmann (Random House, 1974), p. 284.
2 Liang Shuming, *The Substance of Chinese Culture* (Xuelin Publishing, 1987), p. 106.
3 Xu Fuguan, *History of Human Nature in China: The Pre-Qin Period* (Shanghai Joint Publishing, 2001), p. 19.
4 Friedrich Nietzsche, *On the Genealogy of Morals and Ecce Homo*, trans. by Walter Kaufmann and Reginald J. Hollingdale (Random House, 1967), Preface, p. 17.

2 Do the Zhou people's concern-consciousness and respect for virtue constitute a moral breakthrough?

One of the most important contributions made by modern New Confucians, including Mou Zongsan, to describing the moralistic character of Confucianism, consists in claiming a close connection between the origin of Confucianism and the concern-consciousness of the Zhou people, thus relating this consciousness to a kind of moral conscience. Xu Fuguan pointed out that, in Chinese culture, concern-consciousness is crucial for the development from the primitive religion of the Yin and Zhou dynasties to morality. Hence, the Zhou people's concern-consciousness should be interpreted as an "awakening of the humanistic spirit" instead of some kind of "primitive religious motivation." Thus, what this awakening of the humanistic spirit reveals are the spiritual self-awareness, the consciousness and responsibility of the subject rather than the fear and desperation of the primitive religious motivation:

> Concern-consciousness is different from the fear and the desperation peculiar to the primitive religion motivation. In the middle of fear and desperation, people usually feel extremely insignificant, so they give up their duties and make decisions relying on a deity's will. The action is then carried out following the divine will. As for the man himself, this also means that the action deprives him of his own decision and rationality. It may be said, this kind of action is blindly made, without proper moral evaluation. [...] The greatest difference between concern, and fear and desperation, is that the formation of this mental state results from a perspective based on a deep concern of the participants for the auspicious or bad situations, and for success or misfortune. In this perspective, we can see that there is a close relationship between the auspicious or bad situation, the success or misfortune, and who is involved in the activities related to that situation. Moreover, who is involved in that activity is also responsible for the related action. Concern for those people is a mental state related to the unsolved situation of solving the difficulties by their own, and their efforts derive from such a sense of duty. Therefore, concern-consciousness is the direct expression of the sense of responsibility towards things originated by this awakening of humanistic spirit, or

in other words, it is the expression of human self-awareness, which shows itself thanks to the awakening of humanistic spirit.[1]

From Xu Fuguan's perspective, the feature of concern-consciousness highlights the moral obligation of the people involved. In the middle of the fear and desperation of the primitive religious motivation, such a sense of moral obligation is still unseen. In other words, while the awareness of fear and desperation belongs to a belief consciousness peculiar to the primitive religion, concern-consciousness just corresponds to moral conscience. This is because self-confidence and a clear sense of responsibility do not exist in the belief consciousness of primitive religion at all. Only moral conscience embodies those examples of self-confidence and sense of responsibility:

> Under a religious atmosphere with faith as its core, men are saved by faith. When men delegate responsibility for all problems to divinity, the concern-consciousness will not appear. Men's confidence in this situation lies in faith in the divine. Only when someone takes the responsibility for problems does he reveal the concern-consciousness. This concern-consciousness, in fact, embodies a strong will and a fighting spirit.[2]

After establishing concern-consciousness as the main point in his interpretation of moralism, Xu Fuguan further claimed that a fundamental concept in the Zhou people's spiritual world, that is, the concept of *jing* (敬, "respect"), derived from the concern-consciousness. Moreover, since concern-consciousness can be strictly interpreted as a moral conscience, so "respect" can only be explained as *jingde* (敬德, "respect for virtue") and according to "who proceeds to action full of solicitude" (as quoted in *Lunyu* VII.11) in dealing with social relations, instead of a kind of religious reverence:

> Following the active sign of concern-consciousness, the orientation and foundation of human trust gradually shift from referring to divinity to relying on the effort and attentiveness of one's individual behavior. The ideas of *jing* (respect), *jingde* (respect for virtue) and *mingde* (明德, "to manifest the virtue") during the initial first period of the Zhou dynasty reveal the meaning of this attentiveness and effort. In particular, *jing* is what actually exists through people's lifetime. It is a cautious, conscientious psychological attitude based on the watchfulness derived from the concern-consciousness. Through this psychological attitude, men are constantly reflecting on their own behavior and regulating their actions. Despite some similarities, the idea of *jing* stressed during the first period of the Zhou dynasty is different from religious reverence. Religious reverence is a state of mind in which one's subjectivity is annulated, and in which there is a complete devotion to divinity. The idea of *jing* of the first period of the Zhou dynasty highlights a transformation of the human spirit, from being undisciplined to being conscious. In fact, by removing

the desire for an official career from the importance of consciously fulfilling one's duty, it gives prominence to the active, rational and positive
role of one's own subjectivity. The original meaning of the word *jing*
indicated a warning, to be cautious towards an encroachment from outside, and it is a psychological attitude which reflects a passive reaction.
This idea of *jing* of the first period of the Zhou dynasty is instead an inner
and active psychological attitude which includes self-examination. This is
a conscious mental state, totally different from the passive watchful psychological state.[3]

By understanding the concern-consciousness of the Zhou people as a moral
conscience, and then interpreting their idea of *jing* as a moral emotion
instead of a religious emotion, Xu Fuguan explained the fundamental spiritual essence of Confucianism from the stance of moralism. Through this
cohesive philosophical hermeneutic perspective, Xu Fuguan aims to disclose
an illustrious origin for Confucianism instead of an obscure and heteroge-
neous identity.[4] Mou Zongsan further confirmed this point, claiming that
"the focus on the inner moral behavior of Chinese philosophy originates
from the concern-consciousness. Chinese people have a strong sense of
concern-consciousness, and from this concern-consciousness derives moral
conscience."[5] Mou Zongsan not only accepts Xu Fuguan's standpoint about
concern-consciousness, but further develops his argument. First, through the
direct comparison of the Confucian concern-consciousness, the Buddhist
suffering awareness, the Christian sin-consciousness and the related guilty
conscience, he states that "Chinese concern-consciousness is not caused by
the hardship of human life but it stems from a positive moral conscience: it
is a concern for moral cultivation, learning, and practice, and it embodies a
sense of duty."[6] Secondly, he clearly considers the sense of compassion as a
crucial component of concern-consciousness:

> Regardless of how vast and immense Heaven and Earth are, men still find
> something to express their regrets about. Clearly, in the course of life and
> in the universe, there is a regrettable imperfection. So, what about the
> Sage's heart-mind, is it free from this concern? His concern would be on
> the impossibility for the ten thousand creatures to find their *raison d'être*,
> not the fact that they cannot exist and prosper. Becoming pervading and
> extensive, this concern-consciousness results in the notion of the sympa-
> thetic feeling, a sense of compassion towards the world. Compassion is
> the emotion only harbored by idealists. For idealists, compassion itself
> possesses the highest moral value. Despite the greatness of the Heaven
> and Earth, there is still a place for regrets. And towards the ten thousand
> creatures which cannot find their place to be, how is it possible to be indif-
> ferent and have no compassion? Starting from this sense of compassion,
> Confucian thought theorized the idea of actively nourishing all the living
> things in the world and developing inherent participation with Heaven

and Earth. Therefore, *zhi zhonghe* (致中和, "realizing the centered harmony"), so that *tiandi wei* (天地位, "the earth and heaven find their proper places") and *wanwu yu* (万物育, "the ten thousand creatures will be nourished"). Confucian compassion is equivalent to the Buddhist "heart of great compassion" and Christian love. All of these belong to a kind of cosmic feeling.[7]

While Xu Fuguan and Mou Zongsan have not directly defined the concern-consciousness as identical to moral conscience, Li Minghui's statement is more aligned with the definite assertion that "concern-consciousness is indeed a moral conscience."[8] The idea proposed by these three scholars had quite an influence in the Chinese academic world. In his discussion on concern-consciousness, Lin Huowang inherited Xu Fuguan's and Mou Zongsan's views. He summarizes it as "a moral conscience which shows concern about all lives, about people being my brothers and about the life of all creatures."[9] He also explains the meaning of moral conscience as the combination of four different aspects, i.e., self-awareness, being watchful over oneself when alone, sense of compassion and sense of responsibility.[10] It is worth noting that he considers "being watchful over oneself when alone" as a component of the concern-consciousness connotation. This is because Xu Fuguan and Mou Zongsan justified the "appearance of the idea of respect" through the concept of concern-consciousness, and they interpreted the idea of "respect" as a moral emotion, as "respect for virtue" in terms of "proceeding to action full of solicitude" and "being cautious and apprehensive." In the *Doctrine of the Mean*, "being watchful over oneself when alone" is understood as "being cautious and apprehensive," hence it has been possible to use the idea of "being watchful over oneself when alone" when speaking about the concern-consciousness.[11]

It is clear that the moralistic interpretation of concern-consciousness focuses mainly on two aspects: first, it considers that the concern-consciousness indicates the awakening of a human subject's moral conscience, giving prominence to moral self-awareness and sense of responsibility. Furthermore, it holds that the substantial meaning of concern-consciousness is "a sense of compassion possessing the supreme moral value," and it is a concern for all people's lives. In this regard, this cannot but give rise to a doubt: that is, since we understand the concern-consciousness from the standpoint of modern moralism, it might seem to be "revealing the ancient spirit," but, in fact, in the process of this "revelation" we deviate totally from that fundamental ancient spirit. This is because the ancient spirit, perhaps, was extraneous to this "revealing" moralistic claim. Moralism "is always based on what it intends to deduce,"[12] i.e., the interpretation of moralism starts from a designed conclusion in advance and understands that "moral value forms the perspective of behaving actively, doing beneficial actions for others." However, all these spiritual purposes were perhaps entirely unfamiliar to the ancients.

Generally speaking, the origin of concern-consciousness is thought to be closely related to the *Book of Changes*. It is also clearly suggested in the *Great Commentary*:

> Was not he who made Yi familiar with anxiety and calamity?
>
> (*Book of Changes*, Xi Ci II)

> The goings forth and comings in (of lines) are according to rule and measure. People learn from them in external and internal affairs to stand in awe. The book, moreover, makes plain the nature of anxieties and calamities, and the causes of them. Though its students have neither master nor guardian, it is as if their parents draw near to them.
>
> (*Book of Changes*, Xi Ci II)

The *Book of Changes* is a book about divination, so the interpretation of concern-consciousness should be considered from the perspective of the behavior and the psychology directly connected to divination. There are many expressions about good and evil fortune in the *Book of Changes*, like "auspicious," "evil," "advantage," "disadvantage," "regret," "no regret," "death with regrets," "fault," "without faults" and "mean." Zhu Bokun pointed out that apart from the auspicious, the evil, the advantages and disadvantages, other expressions all include the meaning of regret and of renewal.[13] In the *Great Commentary* of the *Book of Changes* (*Xi Ci* II) it is also written that "the good fortune and evil are the indications of the right and wrong (in men's conduct of affairs), and repentance and regret are the indications of their sorrow and anxiety." On this basis, Zhu Bokun considers that the concern-consciousness is "a rational reflection on our sense of terror and crisis" to make people think about potential dangers in a peaceful life and "take great efforts in daily life."[14] This idea, regardless of its moralistic explanation of concern-consciousness, discloses one crucial point, that is, the concern-consciousness is actually closely related to the sense of terror and crisis. Wei Zhengtong also says that concern-consciousness is caused by a "mixture of chaotic and terrified feelings" derived from the sense of duty of the few "leaders with actual group responsibility." For this reason, "it includes a further development than terror."[15] If the concern-consciousness originates from a "sense of terror which is an inherent part of a primitive religion impulse," as claimed by Xu Fuguan, how is the concern-consciousness closely related to the sense of terror? Alternatively, what kind of change happens in the shift from a sense of terror to concern-consciousness? Does it mean a new awakening of moral conscience?

As for the secret psychological relation between the sense of terror and the origin of the divinity, Nietzsche wrote clearly that:

> Within the original tribal community—we are speaking of primeval times—the living generation always recognized a juridical duty toward

earlier generations, and especially toward the earliest, which founded the tribe (and by no means a merely sentimental obligation: there are actually reasons for denying the existence of the latter for the greater part of human history). The conviction reigns that it is only through the sacrifices and accomplishments of the ancestors that the tribe exists—and that one has to pay them back with sacrifices and accomplishments: one thus recognizes a debt that constantly grows greater, since these forebears never cease, in their continued existence as powerful spirits, to accord the tribe new advantages and new strength. ...The fear of the ancestor and his power, the consciousness of indebtedness to him, increases, according to this kind of logic, in exactly the same measure as the power of the tribe itself increases, as the tribe itself grows ever more victorious, independent, honored, and feared. By no means the other way round! ...The ancestors of the most powerful tribes are bound eventually to grow to monstrous dimensions through the imagination of growing fear and to recede into the darkness of the divinely uncanny and unimaginable: in the end the ancestor must necessarily be transfigured into a god. Perhaps this is even the origin of gods, an origin therefore out of fear![16]

When facing the reality of human life experience, as well as life suffering and enjoyment, human rationality initially does not see life circumstances as entirely accidental or untraceable, but instead, it considers them as a process with a reason and an intention. For example, it maintains that there is an external power mastering human life, and this power is deified and endowed with personal features: that is, it is then regarded as a divinity with a willingness and ability to rule human life. In this sense, enjoyments are always explained as a kind of special love or reward from the divinity, while sufferings and disasters are interpreted as a punishment to human beings. The most important feature of this divinity is his immense power: hence, for people, fear is the first emotion caused by the divinity. Naturally, the stronger the deity's power is considered to be, the greater the fear it will impose. If the concern-consciousness is generated by reflection on the sense of fear, there seem to be no spiritual changes during this process, except the change from the external strength inherent in the sense of fear to an internal reminiscence. In a word, the concern-consciousness is nothing but the internalization of the sense of fear. If some psychological relationship surely exists between the sense of fear and the concern-consciousness, it is nothing but fear of punishment. The psychological trait of the fear of punishment plays a crucial role when the external power inherent in the sense of fear turns into the internal concern-consciousness.

The divinity is endowed with personalized features, and it is this divinity who grants sufferings and enjoyments. As a result, sufferings and enjoyments are thought to embody the gods' intention. Since a relation exists between humans and gods, whether humans submit to gods and obey their orders is a fundamental issue. Therefore, sufferings and enjoyments can be considered as the results of submission and obedience to them. The submission and obedience to gods are reflected through men's behavior and their mental state. Hence, the results obtained through the consideration of sufferings and enjoyments, and through the reflection on the sense of fear, shows that there is a specific relationship between the sufferings and enjoyments considered as punishment and reward, the divinity's intention, and men's behavior and human mental states: gods only bless those obedient and punish those disobedient. It is clear that this new recognition of the communication between gods and men became a reasonable life proposition: being obedient to gods for blessings; similarly, being compliant to avoid punishments.

That is, for people this new recognition constitutes a deserved and lasting memory. When men are aware of their behaviors' and attitudes' effects, this gives rise to a kind of self-awareness, probably the self-awareness related to the concern-consciousness. From the psychological aspect of divination, determining the good and evil by divination means to predict gods' intentions. The origin of regret and guilt is to be attributed to men's realization that their behaviors and mental states will have some influence on gods' decisions and, then, they interpret gods' decisions as either punishment or reward for them.

Thus, we can state that the concern-consciousness in fact originates from the psychological fear of punishment. It is the fear of punishment that makes men turn from the external power inherent in the sense of fear to an individual behavior related to a mental state of self-reflection. This internal reflection is self-oriented, that is to say, it concerns the relationship between the inner self and the divinity rather than considering others as external objects. We can even say that, when he is involved in a state of concern-consciousness, every man cares about himself and his relationship with gods rather than the relationship with others. The concern-consciousness is about oneself instead of others or, in other words, considering our fate as a self-concern. Due to the fear of gods' punishment and the self-examination of their behavior, men developed a keen crisis awareness and a concern-consciousness, or, as Mencius wrote in *Mengzi* VIIA.18, "they keep their hearts under a sense of peril and use deep precautions against calamity. On this account they become distinguished for their intelligence."

However, understanding the "self-awareness" related to the concern-consciousness as a kind of "moral awareness" in terms of modern moralism and with an altruistic tendency as the primary spiritual purpose, is to draw a forced conclusion. "Self-awareness" related to the concern-consciousness means "consciously" submitting to the gods' authority. This kind of "self-awareness" is produced under the drive of mental motivation out of the fear of punishment, i.e., forced by the persuasive power of gods.

Similarly, it is also far-fetched to understand the sense of duty related to concern-consciousness as the moral responsibility inherent in modern moralism and analogous to the categorical imperative of practical reason. The sense of duty related to concern-consciousness is actually a burden and a sense of obligation imposed on the human mind, driven by the motivation and derived from terror and fear of punishment. In this sense of duty, men and gods gain a mutual acknowledgment, and it is in this mutual acknowledgment that they gradually build their self-identity.

In the same way, it is inappropriate to directly explain the idea of "respect" generated within the concern-consciousness as equal to the meaning of "proceeding to action full of solicitude" and "being cautious and apprehensive," essential to a moral sense and separated from a religious feeling. Despite the difference between the Zhous' idea of "respect" and the concept of religious reverence, it is still a kind of religious feeling, rather than a moral emotion. The Zhous' idea of "respect" is actually a sense of awe for gods. Besides, this reverence originated from the "sense of awe," that is to say, the feeling of reverence derived from terror at the external higher power of gods. As for the meaning of "respect" inherent in "proceeding to action full of solicitude", we can only understand it from this perspective. As mentioned above, "being cautious and apprehensive" as quoted in the *Doctrine of the Mean* is understood according to the meaning of "proceeding to action full of solicitude" as well. In the *Analects*, Confucius and Zeng Zi used the Classics to explain the necessity of the attitude of "respect" based on "proceeding to action full of solicitude" for social relations:

> Chung-kung asked about perfect virtue. The Master said, "It is, when you go abroad, to behave to everyone as if you were receiving a great guest; to employ the people as if you were assisting at a great sacrifice; not to do to others as you would not wish done to yourself; to have no murmuring against you in the country, and none in the family."[17]
>
> (*Lunyu* XII.2)

> The philosopher Zeng Zi being ill, he cared about the disciples of his school, and said, "Uncover my feet, uncover my hands. It is said in the Book of Poetry, 'We should be apprehensive and cautious, as if on the brink of a deep gulf, as if treading on thin ice, and so have I been.' Now and hereafter, I know my escape from all injury to my person. O ye, my little children."[18]
>
> (*Lunyu* VIII.3)

Here it merely means that the sense of awe for gods should be carried out in all actions, i.e., "proceeding to action full of solicitude" is essentially a religious feeling or, at least, a religious feeling derived from a "sense of awe for gods." There is an essential development or implementation of this religious feeling rather than a radical "moral emotion" or "moral conscience." Tang Junyi wrote, "being cautious and apprehensive in the *Doctrine of the Mean* is a moral character trapped in non-moral emotions and seeking for self-maintaining in moral conscience."[19] If he understands "morality" as an "ontological reality," and "being cautious and apprehensive" as "being cautious and apprehensive within a moral ontology," his interpretation clearly inverts the cause and the effect.

In the academic world, "the secular as sacred" epitomizes the fundamental feature of Confucianism, whereas we may say that "the sacred as the secular" better embodies the spirit of Confucianism. At least, "being cautious and apprehensive" and "proceeding to action full of solicitude" originate from fear towards gods and the sense of awe at the gods' will. If we have to understand "being cautious and apprehensive" and "proceeding to action full of solicitude" as a kind of moral emotion, it should be clear that the proper interpretation of this moral emotion can be understood within a broad religious sphere, like a whole understanding of the Ten Commandments is semantically related to Shangdi's (the Supreme Deity) order. The crucial point here is, the moralistic interpretation of the concern-consciousness considers the moral sense of compassion as an essential connotation of the concern-consciousness idea, and it considers the concern-consciousness as a moral, noble emotion, an "empathetic feeling for others' sufferings and a sympathetic concern for all creatures." However, based on the above analysis, in the concern-consciousness and within the shift from the sense of terror to the concern-consciousness, the primary motive is not a compassion emotion, but a self-oriented thorough consideration directly related to the personal existential situation. Even though there are records about a similar moral emotion in the *Book of Documents*, when the kings concern themselves about the sufferings of the common people "as if they had a serious disease," this point is not relevant in the formation of the concern-consciousness idea, nor in early Confucian thought. However, this does not mean that the concern-consciousness includes no relation with others. We need not deny that it implies a "concern for others." Its moralistic understanding maintains that concern-consciousness is a moral conscience with a direct concern for others and a sense of empathy towards others' sufferings.

In this regard, we have already stated that it is a far-fetched explanation which inverts cause and effect in its argumentation. Since we admit that the concern-consciousness involves a concern for others, it is necessary to explain how the concern-consciousness, which is essentially related to self-concern, involves a concern for others.

When we discuss the concern-consciousness, one key problem we tend to ignore is that it is closely related to a certain status of the person involved. From the historical perspective, the concern-consciousness is linked with men who hold an official post and who take greater responsibility: this responsibility comes from their social status, but not the other way around. In this sense, concern-consciousness includes an intense elitism and, as a result, it implies a concern for others.

We can say that concern-consciousness is fundamentally an ultimate self-concern. What men are concerned about firstly refers to their own destiny and good fortunes, so basically it is a concern about one's actual situation. However, if men who hold official posts are those who hold concerns, their worries for themselves are, at the same time, concerns for their people, since they consider the fortunes of their people as directly determined by their responsibility, and their responsibility originates from their social position. That is to say, their own status requires them to take the good fortunes of the people as their duty. So, in this kind of concern-consciousness, which includes an ultimate self-concern, even concerns for the world still belong to their own duty. The concern for others stems from a primary personal sense of duty which is closely related to a social status and determined by that status: it is not based on moral sympathetic emotion. Giving up this duty means giving up on oneself. It is thus clear that understanding the concern-consciousness from the self-concern point of view is considerably different from directly explaining it as moral conscience. In other words, despite the fact that an altruistic consideration can be inferred from the concern-consciousness, that consideration is neither the root of the concern-consciousness nor the main intent. The reduction of concern-consciousness to moral conscience not only conceals the actual origin of the concern-consciousness but also changes its essential nature. The idea that Confucian concern-consciousness leads to moral autonomy more than to the consciousness inspired by the sense of awe of a religious faith (for example in Christianity), is an apparently right but actually wrong conclusion on the part of modern humanism. In fact, modern ideas and practices including moral autonomy arose in the Christian world where social life was enveloped by religious faith. For Confucius, the founder of Confucianism wrongly considered a humanist, reverence for "the fate decided by Heaven" is still a key point.

Besides, in order to distinguish the concern-consciousness and the religious consciousness in a hermeneutical perspective on moralism, Xu Fuguan and Mou Zongsan both deemed that the concern-consciousness cannot derive from the devotion of religious belief. This view is also controversial. If men who hold official posts believe that the responsibility for their people's good fortunes originates from gods' orders or because of their duty, the sincerer this belief is, the stronger their concern-consciousness will become. In other words, with a clearer self-understanding, they tend to have a more definite awareness of their identity, of their necessary duty regulated by their status, and this perhaps generates a stronger concern-consciousness. The concern-consciousness and sincere faith not only have no contradictory relationship but a constructive and mutual connection. Here, the misunderstanding of Xu Fuguan and Mou Zongsan is that they understood the concern-consciousness starting from a predetermined moralistic view.

Looking for an "illustrious moral origin" for Confucian thought, the moralistic Confucians not only explained the concern-consciousness as the seed of moral conscience, but also explained the respect for virtue, or the Zhou concept—represented by the Duke of Zhou as *yi de pei Tian* (以德配天, "to complete and be in accord to Heaven with virtue")—as a moral breakthrough. They argue that the idea of "to complete and be in accord to Heaven with virtue" allows the Zhou people to build moral authority in their spiritual world, and further turn their comprehension of Heaven's will into a moralistic view with self-awareness, altruism and vivid humanism. Thus, the ideas of *ming de shen fa* (明德慎罚, "promoting virtue and being prudent in the infliction of punishment") and *jing de bao min* (敬德保民, "worshipping virtue, protecting the people") advocated by the Zhou people can be properly interpreted within this moralistic framework.

The idea of virtue has an early origin, tracing back to the period prior to the Xia, Shang and Zhou dynasties. From the perspective of the current literature, in the *Book of Documents* "virtue," on one hand, is not only a key concept in the *Book of Zhou*, but also quite common in other books; on the other hand, according to many scholars doing academic research in ancient writing, the character *de* (virtue) has been found both in bronze inscriptions and in oracle bone inscriptions.[20] Nevertheless, the importance of "virtue" is part of the Zhou dynasty, which best presents the features of Zhou people's ideas compared with those of the Yin-Shang period.

The importance of the concept of "virtue" during the Zhou dynasty is closely related to Zhou people's legitimate basic argument for the radical change of political power and their decision to overthrow the Yin-Shang dynasty. Commonly, it is said that people in the Yin-Shang dynasty already have the idea of the Supreme Deity separated from the ancestors' spiritual beings. In their life, an important religious belief is that "the deceased father and the departed king serve the god." People in the Yin-Shang dynasty believe that the deceased ancestors ("the deceased father and the departed king") go to Heaven and they can be welcomed by the Supreme Deity or receive a high official position, i.e., "serve the Supreme Deity as attendants."[21]

Hence, concerning the communication between the king, i.e., the head of the ancestral descendants in the human world, and the Supreme Deity, ancestors play a crucial role. As a tribal family head, the king's relationship with the Supreme Deity also represents the tribe's relationship with the Supreme Deity. More directly, good fortunes of future generations depend, to a great extent, on the ancestors' blessing through a direct communication with the Supreme Deity. Crucial evidence is that divination in the Yin people's daily life always resorts to their ancestors for any inquiry:

> From the oracle inscriptions, we can see that prediction by divining is not carried on by directly asking the Supreme Deity; neither a prediction on the activity of river gods or ghosts involves a direct inquiry of the river gods or ghosts. Questions asked of the Supreme Deity, the spiritual beings or the ghosts concerning something haunted, or something that has bad influence, can be seen through oracle inscriptions. Therefore, divination is to inquire through ancestors by a mysterious method based on the idea that the god of ancestors will give responses through a cracking tortoise shell.[22]

We can assume that, based on their faith system and sacrifice system, only through one's ancestors can the will of the Supreme Deity be understood. In the Yin dynasty's spiritual world, the issue of Heaven's commands, in a political context and concerning all fortunes of future generations, relies on ancestors. Nonetheless, we should not misread the spiritual world of Yin people as shrouded by fatalism and paying no attention to men's practical ability. Supposing that most records in the *Book of Documents* are authentic, although the Zhou people have revised many contents, *de* (virtue) is quite significant in the Yin people's spiritual world and the attention to virtue might be traced back to an earlier period.

Related to this is the religious phenomenon of *Shangdi bu xiang si* (上帝不享祀, "the Supreme Deity will not take part in the sacrificial offerings"). In the Yin and Zhou dynasties, sacrifice is a matter of prime importance in people's lives. From the perspective of its effective function, sacrifice is, first of all, an action to attract good fortune and avoid misfortunes, asking for Heaven's blessings. However, regarding the sacrificial offerings, a widespread idea during the Yin and Zhou periods was that "the Supreme Deity will not take part in the sacrificial offerings," but in comparison, to offer sacrifice to ancestors was extremely solemn. From the oracle bone inscriptions of the Yin Ruins we can see that, for Yin Dynasty people in particular, sacrifice to ancestors was rather grand but the Supreme Deity was not the target of the sacrifice.[23] If the one who grants good or evil fortunes is the Supreme Deity, why do descendants in the human world ask for blessings through sacrificing to ancestors, and not directly perform an offering sacrifice to the Supreme Deity? The reason is that ancestors partake in their descendants' sacrifice because of their mutual blood relations, while the gods, as the Supreme Deity, "will not take part in the sacrifice" because there is no certain blood relation with any specific tribe. This is what is reported in *Zuo's Commentary*, with these two passages: "Ghosts and gods who don't belong to a tribe don't partake in his sacrifice" and "gods do not take part in what is of a different kind, and people do not sacrifice to different tribal clans." This idea has a long history, and even Confucius (see *Lunyu* II.24) said that for a man to sacrifice to a spirit which does not belong to him is flattery. Although the related literature still remains insufficient, we can still assert that, from the fact that the Yin people had faith in the Supreme Deity but at the same time gave importance to ancestors, performing sacrifices for ancestors rather than to the Supreme Deity, filial piety definitely plays a significant role in their lives. There are records in the *Book of Documents* about the order given by the Emperor Shun to Xie, saying as follows:

> Xie, the people are still wanting in affection for one another, and do not docilely observe the five orders of relationship. It is yours, as the Minister of Instruction, reverently to set forth the lessons of duty belonging to those five orders. Do so with gentleness.

In the *Mengzi* IIIA it is also said that:

> this was a subject of anxious solicitude to the sage Shun, and he appointed Xie to be the Minister of Instruction, to teach the relations

of humanity: how, between father and son, there should be affection; between husband and wife, attention to their separate functions; between old and young, a proper order; and between friends, fidelity.

However, in *Zuo's Commentary* it is said that "acknowledging allegiance to Yao, the Emperor Shun praises the Eight Worthies and preaches the Five teachings to the world, including a father's righteousness, a mother's kindness, an older brother's friendliness, a younger brother's respect and a son's filial piety." Based on past research, the "five moral values" and the "five teachings" refer to the five cardinal relationships that virtue ethics required. Among them, filial piety corresponds to the relationship between father and son and it has quite an importance.[24] It is worth pointing out that filial piety not only refers to the relationship between offspring and their parents but also the relationship between descendants and their ancestors. Taking some expressions of later literature as our reference, we can say that filial piety not only means treating parents kindly, including providing support, love and respect, but also reveals a feeling ensuring that men pay debts of gratitude to ancestors and pay careful attention to their parents' funerary rites: this means that filial piety not only is related to the ethical concept of family and clan but also refers to ethical ideas of religion and politics. In the Yin people's spiritual world, ancestors play an important intermediary role in the communication between descendants and the spiritual beings, and the legitimate idea of politics stems from religious belief. For instance, there is a passage in the *Book of Documents* which says: "In serving the ancestors, first reflect on filial piety." In another passage, the Duke of Zhou accused the Yin people of "no filial piety and friendliness." In *Master Lü's Spring and Autumn Annals* it is said that "in the Book of Documents is reported that 'three hundred kinds of criminal punishments are all no more severe than that for conducts of no filial piety.'" These works all make clear from different perspectives that the Yin people's filial piety exceeds the ethics of family and clan.

When the small Zhou state overthrew the large state of Yin, the Zhou people faced the issue of a legitimate argument for their political power. In pleading this legitimate basis, the meaning of virtue became prominent. In the Zhou people's spiritual world, closely connected with this legitimation quest was the crucial idea of the "uncertainty of Heaven's mandate." We must recognize that the insufficient literature makes it challenging to provide a final assertion and a vivid description of the Yin people's understanding of the ownership of Heaven's commands in the sense of politics and moral edification. However, we can generally deduct that "the uncertainty of Heaven's mandate" is a quite peculiar idea in the Zhou people's spiritual world compared with that of the Yin people, or, at least, it is an idea which receives particular attention from the Zhou people. This idea is directly related to the legitimation of the Zhou people's political revolution because this legitimation issue at that time was indeed a problem of ownership of Heaven's mandate. What needs to be pointed out is, supposing that the Zhou idea of the "uncertainty of Heaven's mandate" reflects some doubts on the matter related to Heaven, they question the certainty of Heaven's mandate rather than its existence. According to those modern scholars who embrace a humanistic standpoint (if involved in the moralistic understanding of Confucianism), they see here the striving of a humanistic spirit: without adding any further explanation, this is merely a far-fetched interpretation. Since the ownership of Heaven's mandate can change, what needs to be predicted and understood is whether this change has some rules. The Zhou people make the meaning of virtue prominent in this context. In other words, Zhou people think that, as for the issue of the ownership of Heaven's mandate, the crucial variable is virtue: only those possessing virtue can own and keep Heaven's mandate, or vice versa. This not only means that cultivating virtue is the only way to gain access to Heaven's mandate, but also indicates that those who possess virtue are able to carry out a legitimate political revolution and replace the government of those without virtue. This is called *gong xing tian zhi fa* (恭行天之罚, "reverently executing the punishment appointed by Heaven"), as seen in many passages of the *Book of Documents*. In this sense, virtue refers in fact to the relationship of a tribe with Heaven, both tracing back to ancestors and extending to their descendants, or precisely speaking, the relationship between the king as the tribal leader and Heaven.[25] In summary, the idea of how to keep Heaven's mandate interpreted through the importance of virtue by the Zhou people is also the idea related to the legitimation of a political revolution. Zhou people describe the ancient Golden age and explain the substitution and changes of Xia, Shang and Zhou Dynasties according to this idea, further creating a legitimate argument for their revolution, and this is what is meant by *Zhou sui jiu bang, qi ming wei xin* (周虽旧邦，其命惟新, "despite being an old nation, Zhou's mission is to make innovation").

Since virtue is, therefore, the most important variable regarding the ownership of Heaven's mandate, the respect for virtue (*jingde*), instead of ancestors' blessings, is a priority in order to keep Heaven's mandate. We see in fact that no matter when the idea of virtue originates and whether it is related to filial piety, the importance of virtue for the Zhou people is highlighted in comparison with filial piety, at least on the ethical level of religion and politics:

> Great Heaven has no partial affections; it helps only the virtuous.
> (*Book of Documents*, "Charge to Cai Zhong")

> Ever think of your ancestor, cultivating your virtue, always striving to accord with Heaven's mandate, so shall you be seeking for much happiness.
> (*Book of Songs*, Greater Odes of the Kingdom, Wen Wang)

The meaning of filial piety, from "serving the parents" by extension came to mean "showing gratitude and cherishing the memory of ancestors." However, the sayings *Huangtian wu qin* (黄天无亲, "Great Heaven has no partial affections") and *wu nian er zu* (无念尔祖, "do not ever think of your ancestor") indicate that, in order to keep Heaven's mandate, people did not place their hope on ancestors anymore, but aimed to acquire Heaven's blessing thanks to their virtue. In other words, the meaning of virtue reveals itself through the comparative narration of filial piety connected to "serving the parents and remembering the ancestors": filial piety corresponds to the relationship between the descendants (always referring to a tribe, represented by their tribe leader, a king) and the ancestors, that is, the relationship between men and ancestry. Virtue corresponds instead to the relationship between a tribe, or the king of a tribe, and Heaven, so it is the relationship between men and Heaven.

What we have just stated does not mean that in the period before the Zhou, characterized by a great solemnity in celebrating the ancestors, virtue had no importance. Moreover, there is definitely no reason to argue that the Zhou people created the idea of virtue, nor that filial piety became less important after the attention paid to virtue established by the Zhou people. This point reminds us that, regarding the political revolution at the time of the Yin and Zhou dynasties, which exerted great historical influence and brought relevant changes to the social system and spiritual world of that time, we must maintain a balanced point of view, without omitting or overstating this fact.[26] The fact is, regardless of whether the aspect under consideration is related to the social system or to the spiritual world, the Zhou culture shows some continuity compared with cultures of earlier times, and also reveals its innovative character thanks to the effect of its transformation.

Regarding the passage "Great Heaven has no partial affections and helps only the virtuous," there are some records in the *Book of Documents* (precisely in the *Tai Jia* chapter) with a similar expression:

> Yi Yin again made an announcement to the king, saying, "Oh! Heaven has no (partial) affection—only to those who are reverent does it show affection. The people are not constant to those whom they cherish; they cherish (only) him who is benevolent. The spirits do not always accept the sacrifices that are offered to them; they accept only the sacrifices of the sincere."

It is clear that there is no difference between "Heaven has no (partial) affection" seen in the in *Tai Jia* chapter, and "Great Heaven has no partial affections" recorded in the "Charge to Cai Zhong." The only difference is, in the *Tai Jia* chapter, the crucial point of intimate bond and the submission to Heaven lies in reverence or honesty, while in the "Charge to Cai Zhong" chapter this relies on virtue. In addition, as mentioned above, we can see that starting from the *Book of Shang* section of the *Book of Documents* and even earlier, the origin of "virtue" can be traced back to an earlier time. If we check the literary context concerning the Zhou people's attention to filial piety, we can see many references in the *Book of Zhou* section of the *Book of Documents*, as well as in the *Book of Songs*:

If you can cultivate your milles and hasten about in the service of your fathers and elders; and if with your carts and oxen, you traffic diligently to a distance, that you may thereby filially minister to your parents.

(*Book of Documents*, "The Announcement about Drunkenness")

In order that you many cover the faults of your father, be loyal, be filial. Urge on your steps in your own way, diligent and never idle, and so shall you hand down an example to your descendants.

(*Book of Documents*, "The Charge to Cai Zhong")

Ever thinking how to be filial; His filial mind was the model [which he supplied]. (*Book of Songs*, Major Odes)

We can see that in the spiritual world of the Zhou people, although virtue is a religious and political ethical core concept, its importance can be highlighted through a comparison with filial piety. However, on the level of religious and political ethics, the Zhou people see virtue and filial piety as equally significant, even stressing the importance of filial piety on the level of family clan ethics. Hou Wailu wrote: "Zhou people pay equal attention to virtue and filial piety, complying to Heaven with virtue and with filial piety to ancestors."[27] Explaining in few words the meaning of Zhou rites, Chen Lai said:

Within a social framework, Zhou rites consolidate the religious and legal order, cultivate life regulations within the clan and strengthen the cohesion inside the clan. All these aspects can be summed up in one word, "filial piety." In this sense, "filial piety" not only refers to the filial support for parents but represents the universal value of the clan's interest, order and proliferation.[28]

Since the difference between virtue and filial piety is that the former corresponds to the relationship between the clan, or the king as the leader of a clan, and Heaven, while the latter corresponds to the relationship between the descendants and the forefathers and ancestors, i.e., the relationship between men and ancestry, so, what is the relation between virtue and filial piety? There is one reason for mentioning this issue: in the ancient literature, it is common to find that, particularly as the rank of a clan's king is concerned, the descendants always mention the word "virtue" relating to ancestors' exhortations. For example, in the "Charge to the Count of Wei" chapter of the *Book of Documents*, where the King of Cheng appoints the Count of Wei as lord of Song to lead the Yin people, it is said:

Examining into antiquity, (I find) that the honoring of the virtuous (belongs to their descendants) who resemble them in worth, and (I appoint) you to continue the line of the kings your ancestors, observing their ceremonies and taking care of their various relics. Come (also) as a guest to our royal House, and enjoy the prosperity of our kingdom, for ever and ever without end. "Oh! Your ancestor, Tang the Successful, was reverent and sage, (with a virtue) vast and deep. The favor and help of great Heaven lighted upon him, and he grandly received its appointment, to soothe the people by his gentleness, and remove the wicked oppressions from which they were suffering. His achievements affected his age, and his virtue was transmitted to his posterity. And you are the one who pursues and cultivates his plans; this praise has belonged to you for long. Reverently and carefully have you discharged your filial duties; gravely and respectfully you behave to spirits and to men."

From the literature cited here and other many works, we can see that, as far the relationship between the king and the ancestors is concerned, virtue is always quite significant: the reason why cultivating virtue became part of ancestors' regular exhortations, is because, first of all, ancestors have achieved this virtue, and thus they received Heaven's commands. Hence, in those descendants' view, complying with the ancestors' exhortations and cultivating the virtue according to the ancestors' example is the perfect way to display filial piety and preserve Heaven's mandate.[29] In fact, since the relationship between a king and Heaven represents the relationship between the tribe led by him and Heaven, then this relationship also involves that tribe's ancestors. That is to say, the relationship between the tribe and Heaven is diachronic, involving the tribe's king of that time, as well as the ancestors and descendants of the tribe. In this diachronic context, in order to have and maintain Heaven's mandate, a tribe, first of all, relies on the ancestors' cultivation of virtue, and then relies on the virtue achievements obtained at that time or by later generations, thus constantly attempting the cultivation of virtue.[30] In other words, virtue, as a collective property passed from generation to generation, is not fixed but can be accumulated and can be reduced. To accumulate and increase virtue is the flourishing way, for the tribe, to keep Heaven's mandate, while losing virtue is the dangerous way for a tribe to ruin Heaven's mandate. On the other hand, for the descendants, if maintaining Heaven's mandate is the proper manifestation of their filial piety towards their ancestors, then the cultivation of virtue can be reasonably seen as the proper conduct of filial piety.[31]

Clarifying the comparison and the mutual relation between virtue and filial piety helps us to understand the context highlighted by this notion of virtue. Then, how do we understand the inner connotation of virtue? In the academic world, there are controversial opinions concerning the origin of the idea of virtue,[32] but there is one point on which scholars have reached an agreement, that is, a proper understanding of the notion of virtue of the early literary works can be fully acquired in a religious context, i.e., virtue is a purely religious concept. This is consistent with our analysis, as mentioned earlier, on "complying to Heaven with virtue and complying to ancestors with filial piety," and to the mutual involvement of virtue and filial piety. Besides, although the exegetical interpretation of *de zhe, de ye* (德者，得也,

"to be virtuous, is to obtain") is a late phenomenon, there is no reason to doubt it. On the contrary, the reasonableness of this exegetical interpretation is quite evident: since virtue corresponds to the relationship between man and Heaven, people who receive an assignment from Heaven—and comparatively it is Heaven that confers it—those people then obtain Heaven's mandate. Therefore, concerning the interpretation of the relationship between man and Heaven, the exegetical explanation linking *de* (virtue) with *de* (to obtain) constitutes a quite reasonable hermeneutical circle. Based on these two points and taking reference from other opinions in the academic world, we can draw the general outline of virtue's origin. First, the earlier origin of virtue might be related to a descent of spiritual beings within a shamanic practice, like a séance. As a way of communication between men and Heaven, séances include many features, such as possession and related rituals. In this regard, although individual shamans conduct séances, séances are always a group activity related to some common issues of a tribe. Moreover, the exegetical linking of *de* (virtue) with *de* (to obtain) is quite meaningful here, since it "obtained (or possessed) by the god."[33] Secondly, since virtue is concerned with the tribal group life and the authority over interpreting Heaven's commands belongs to the shaman, then, virtue might mean that a tribe is endowed with special favor and a special mission by Heaven. This connotation is still closely related to two points mentioned above: as for the former, virtue directly involves the relation between the tribe and Heaven and is further related to ancestors and descendants. As for the latter, virtue indicates that the tribe receives special favor and a peculiar mission from Heaven.[34] Thirdly, in the context of a séance, virtue is carried out by the particular individual presence of the shaman. Perhaps through an evolution of this fact (i.e., that virtue is related to some select individuals appointed by Heaven), the shamans in the beginning, and later the tribal leaders or the king, are endowed with special favor and granted with a mission as awards with certain conditions. Similarly, this interpretation is closely connected to two points mentioned before: as for the former, virtue directly indicates the relationship between the king and Heaven; as for the latter, virtue means the special favor and the unique mission Heaven granted to the king. Furthermore, the meaning of virtue might evolve from some unique ability granted to some select individuals to the ability to be appointed with Heaven's mandate.[35] At this point, the meaning of virtue is similar to the idea of virtue of the Zhou people and their later generations.

We can see from the Zhou people's thought that kings are those unique individuals who receive a special favor and a singular mission and are equipped with exceptional ability to carry Heaven's mandate. Specifically, kings are *yuanhou* (元后, "great sovereigns") who assist and help the Supreme Deity and who act as people's fathers-and-mothers in the vast world:

> Heaven and earth are the parents of all creatures; and of all creatures man is the most highly endowed. The sincerely intelligent (among men)

becomes the great sovereign; and the great sovereign is the parent of the people.

> (*Book of Documents*, "The Great Declaration")

Heaven, for the help of the inferior people, made for them rulers, and made for them instructors, that they might be able to aiding God, and secure the tranquility of the four quarters (of the kingdom).

> (*Book of Documents*, "The Great Declaration")

In the Book of History it is said, "Heaven having produced the inferior people, made for them rulers and teachers, with the purpose that they should assist God, and therefore distinguished them throughout the four quarters of the land. Whoever are offenders, and whoever are innocent, here am I to deal with them. How dare any under Heaven give indulgence to their refractory wills?"

> (*Mengzi* IB)

Virtue is a conditional favor granted by Heaven to kings, probably including a unique ability to receive Heaven's commands and a social status related to the favor accorded to the individual and the tribe, while the practical requirement lies in "being people's fathers-and-mothers."[36] In a word, protecting his people is a special favor and unique mission endowed by Heaven on a king. For the king who receives such favor and mission, protecting people is his essential duty, showing reverence and obedience to Heaven, and the best way to guarantee his position and good fortune.[37] This is the idea of "complying to the status with virtue." In this sense, *jingde* (respect for virtue) refers to respect for Heaven, and at the same time, it means protection for people. Similarly, *mingde* (to manifest the virtue) indicates understanding Heaven and showing affection to the people. The unique ability granted to the king by Heaven, according to the cited literature, generally refers to *cong ming* (聪明, "insight"). We need to point out that in later times, particularly in our current context, one who possesses insight is always considered to have some talent other than virtue; this contains no religious meaning. But in the context of the Zhou people, insight, without any doubt, belongs to virtue and virtue here is, first of all, a religious concept.[38] If it is related to the Zhou people's two common sayings, i.e., *jingde* (respect for virtue) and *mingde* (to manifest the virtue), then having insight (as "to hear" and "to grasp" clearly) is basically parallel to *jingde* and *mingde*. While "to hear" pays more attention to the former, "to grasp" stresses the latter. Thus, the parallelism between "to hear" and "to grasp," and the idea of "what Heaven hears is what my people hear and what Heaven sees is what my people see" is quite apparent.

In the current literature, some evidence can be found about the idea that virtue is regarded as the unique ability endowed by Heaven to kings as a way to receive Heaven's mandate. For example, in the *Book of Documents* (in the "Announcement of Zhonghui") it is reported that the sovereign of Xia had his virtue all-obscured, and the people were (as if they had fallen) amid mire and (burning) charcoal. Heaven hereupon gifted (our) king with valor and prudence, to serve as a sign and director to the myriad regions

in which "valor and prudence" refers exactly to the virtue endowed by Heaven. Another example lies in the "Tai Jia" chapter of the *Book of Documents*:

The former king kept his eye continually on the bright requirements of Heaven, and so he maintained the worship of the spirits of Heaven and Earth, of those presiding over the land and the grain, and of those of the ancestral temple—all with a sincere reverence. Heaven took notice of his virtue, and caused its great appointment to light on him, that he should soothe and tranquillize the myriad regions.

Here "virtue" also means "the illustrious Heaven's mandate." In the *Great Learning* the words "the ancestor obeys the illustrious Heaven's mandate" are cited to explain the meaning of *ming mingde* (明明德, "manifesting one's bright virtue"): Zhu Xi explains the so-called "illustrious Heaven's mandate" as "the reason why Heaven bestows is myself, and the reason why I act is virtue." To a certain extent, it means that Heaven grants some special ability to people. The so-called "manifesting one's bright virtue" indicates that people understand and fully employ these special abilities endowed by Heaven.

When virtue is seen as a unique ability granted by Heaven, the relationship between virtue and human nature is rather obvious, because human nature refers actually to the inner nature (what we are born with is our nature) or destiny ("What Heaven confers" is called "nature"). This can only be related to a further development of the concept of virtue. When in *Lunyu* Confucius says, "Heaven produced the virtue that is in me," he already puts in evidence the real connotation of virtue. In his vivid description of the separation between shamanic practice and virtuous conduct, Confucius, to some extent, has shown the secret origin of virtue:

The praise failing to reach the number is called witchcraft. The number failing to reach the virtue is called history [...] My quest is only for virtue, and my purpose and path are different from the one which belongs to the divinatory shamanic practice. The superior man in his virtuous conduct ask for blessings, so the sacrifice offerings are few. Who by practising the benevolence asks for favor, so he chooses less to use divination.

The *Record of Music* also says that "virtue is the beginning of human nature." The *Doctrine of the Mean* also places "virtue" and "nature" in an equal position: "The superior man honors his virtuous nature and maintains constant inquiry and study." Clearly, it expresses the idea of the virtuous receiving Heaven's command and the way to comply to his position with virtue:

> Therefore having such great virtue, it could not but be that he should obtain the throne, that he should obtain those riches, that he should obtain his fame, and that he should attain to his long life. Thus it is that Heaven, in the production of things, is sure to be bountiful to them, according to their qualities. Hence the tree that is flourishing is nourished, while that which is ready to fall is overthrown. In the *Book of Poetry*, it is said, "The admirable amiable prince displayed conspicuously his excelling virtue, correcting his people, and correcting his officers. Therefore, he received from Heaven his emoluments of dignity. It protected him, assisted him, and decreed to him the throne; sending from Heaven these favors, as it were repeatedly." We may say therefore that he who is greatly virtuous will be sure to receive the appointment of Heaven.

Therefore, it can be said that "what Heaven has conferred is called nature" in the first chapter of the *Doctrine of the Mean* actually means "what Heaven has conferred is called virtue" and is the inheritance and development of the Zhou people's idea of virtue. The concept of nature related to the idea of *weifa zhi zhong* (未发之中, "not yet expressed centrality," i.e., in an equilibrium state of mind under unstirred pleasure, anger, sorrow or joy) could also be understood in this context. When speaking about the thought of the pre-Qin period, it is always mentioned that:

> what people receive from the Earth and Heaven and what they are born with, it is their fate. Actions, behaviors, rules of rites are those which define this fate. Those who can live with it have good fortunes, while those who fail have evil fortunes.
>
> (quoted in *Zuo's Commentary on Spring and Autumn Annals*)

If we connect these words with the idea of virtue as the illustrious Heaven's command, and if we consider the Zhou people's idea of virtue as the way to ask for favor and to avoid evil fortunes, it is easy to understand that virtue, as the beginning part of human nature, represents the basis for people's comprehension, approval and development of the fate endowed by Heaven, that is, it is the cardinal principle of the universe. Mencius used words from the *Book of Songs* to explain the idea of the "goodness of human nature": "Heaven, in giving birth to the multitudes of the people, to every faculty and relationship annexed its law. The people possess this normal nature, and they [consequently] love its normal virtue." According to Mencius' interpretation, "normal virtue" refers to the pure and perfectly good nature endowed by Heaven. From this, we can see that, although we usually think that Mencius set the basis for the idea of the goodness of human nature, this idea still has its origin. More directly, Mencius' theory of the goodness of human nature developed from the concept of virtue of the Zhou people.[39]

Since the virtuous one is the person who has been granted a special favor and unique mission by Heaven and endowed with exceptional ability to receive a mandate, the virtuous one represents a purely religious idea. By using the current philosophical definition, the virtuous one refers to one who is a transcendental agent, because he has been endowed with transcendental agency. Considering that in his activity (as the "great virtue of Heaven and Earth is creating life") Heaven favored those individuals with this transcendental agency, and if this, for those individuals, is a favorable bestowal, the transcendental agency received from Heaven is, in fact, an immanent grace.

Furthermore, considering the later development of the Zhou people's concept of virtue, Heaven, in his creative activity, universally endowed everyone with transcendental agency. We can then conclude—on the basis of either what is said in the *Doctrine of the Mean*, i.e., "what Heaven has conferred is called nature," or what the *Mengzi* reports, i.e., "benevolence, rites and wisdom are all inherent in me"—that this means the following most religious idea is generated consistently from the Zhou interpretation of virtue. Everyone is favored with an immanent endowment in the creative activity of Heaven and Earth: this is human nature. It is in this sense we should not consider the idea of human nature of Confucius' and Mencius' thought as equal to the human nature of Western thought, no matter whether derived from the Greek or from the Judeo-Christian philosophical tradition.

From the analysis expounded above, we can see that intended as the transcendental agency or immanent endowment, virtue is far different from the virtue of modern moralism, and it is significantly different from the concept of *arête* based on the natural teleology of Greek philosophy. Although in the early stage of Confucian thought the appearance and development of the idea of virtue are groundbreaking, particularly if compared with the earlier shamanic tradition, we cannot reasonably accept the far-fetched moralistic interpretation of virtue as modern humanism's fundamental aim. Nevertheless, it is not pointless to reductively explain the Zhou people's idea of virtue and its later Confucian development as a moralistic concept. From some reasoning perspectives, although the Zhou people's idea of virtue is a purely religious concept and the following Confucian idea of virtue is different from a moralistic or inherently altruistic connotation of virtue, it is, however, possible to recognize an inherent altruistic tendency, both in the Zhou people's and Confucians' ideas. As far the Zhou people are concerned, being the virtuous one who receives special favor and a unique mission from Heaven, the king's duty is to rule as people's father-and-mother. If we focus on the particular relationship between the king and the people, understood as a relationship between parents and sons (and thus from here derive the saying "protecting the people like a newborn child"), and, at the same time, we apply an abstract reasoning to it, we can see that the people can be seen as an "other," so the moralistic interpretation of virtue is quite evident. As for Confucianism in the later period, if we apply the same abstract understanding to virtue given by Heaven (like benevolence, rites and wisdom), in other words, if we put aside the hierarchical order (where family order plays a fundamental role) which finds correspondence with benevolence, rites and wisdom, then the moralistic interpretation of virtue can be achieved. The reductive moralistic interpretation of the Zhou people's idea of virtue, and of the concept of virtue arising in the later classical period of Confucianism, only seems to be well-grounded. Actually, it entirely removes the basis of existence; it is a hidden way to subvert the ethical structure of the classical period, including the self, the family, the nation, the world and even the universe.

Notes

1 Xu Fuguan, *History of Human Nature in China: The Pre-Qin Period* (Shanghai Joint Publishing, 2001), pp. 18–19.
2 Xu Fuguan, *History of Human Nature in China*, p. 20.
3 Xu Fuguan, *History of Human Nature in China*, p. 20.
4 Foucault pointed out that Nietzsche distinguishes the notions of "origin" *(Ursprung)* and "background" (*Herkunft*) in the book *On the Genealogy of Morals*. The word "origin" assumes some homogeneity between the words "source" and "flow," and it has a philosophical hermeneutical target which relies on the "flow" tracing back to the "source," while the "background" focuses on the heterogeneity between the "source" and the "flow," always trying to trace back, and results in the hidden changeable power within the source and the course. In trying to trace back to an inherently different origin, it is the "grey part" of the genealogical work. See Michel Foucault, "Nietzsche, Genealogy, History" (trans. by Su Li), in Liu Xiaofeng and Ni Weiguo (eds.), *Nietzsche in the West* (Shanghai Joint Publishing, 2002).
5 Mou Zongsan, *Features of Chinese Philosophy* (Shanghai Ancient Books, 1977), p. 12.
6 Mou Zongsan, *Features of Chinese Philosophy*, p. 16. In his idea he quoted the words of Confucius (*Lunyu* VII.3):

> That I fail to cultivate Virtue, that I fail to inquire more deeply into that which I have learned, that upon hearing what is right I remain unable to move myself to do it, and that I prove unable to reform when I have done something wrong—such potential failings are a source of constant worry to me.
>
> (Trans. by Edward G. Slingerland, in Philip J. Ivanhoe and Bryan W. Van Norden (eds.), *Readings in Classical Chinese Philosophy* (Hackett, 2005), p. 20)

7 Mou Zongsan, *Features of Chinese Philosophy* (Shanghai Ancient Books, 1997), pp. 12–13.
8 Li Minghui, "On the so-called 'Confucian Extensive Moralism,'" in *Confucianism and Modern Sense* (Wen Jin Press, 1911), p. 67.
9 Lin Huowang, *On Knowledge and Behavior from Confucian Concern-Consciousness* (Zhengzhong Book Press, 1981), p. 11.
10 Lin Huowang, *On Knowledge and Behavior*, p. 23 et seq.
11 Lin Huowang, *On Knowledge and Behavior*, p. 26 et seq.

12 See Max Scheler's criticism of sympathy ethics in *The Nature of Sympathy*, selected from Liu Xiaofeng (ed.), *Collected Works of Max Scheler*, Vol. 1 (Shanghai Joint Publishing, 1999), pp. 277–314. For bringing order to the issues related to the Christian spiritual world, thanks to the inspiration given by Nietzsche's thought, Scheler is called "the Christian Nietzsche," which is quite enlightening for us.

13 Zhu Bokun, *Concern-Consciousness and the Ethnical Spirit of the Book of Changes*, 1st ed. (Journal of Peking University, 1997).

14 Zhu Bokun, *Concern-Consciousness and the Ethnical Spirit*, pp. 96–100.

15 Wei Zhengtong, *Research on Chinese Philosophical Origins from the Book of Changes*, cited in Lin Huowang, *On Knowledge and Behavior*, p. 16.

16 Friedrich Nietzsche, *On the Genealogy of Morals and Ecce Homo*, trans. by Walter Kaufmann and Reginald J. Hollingdale (Random House, 1967), Second Essay, Section 19, pp. 88–89.

17 "Your humble servant was told that 'when you go abroad, behave to everyone as if you were receiving a great guest; employ the people as if you were assisting at a great sacrifice. This is the standard of benevolence.'" *Zuo's Commentary on Spring and Autumn Annals.*

18 The poem cited is from the *Book of Poetry.*

19 Tang Junyi, *On the Origin of Chinese Philosophy: Introduction* (Xinya Academy Research Institute, 1974), p. 133.

20 Many scholars believe that oracle inscription of *zhi* (值) is the archaic form of the character "virtue" (*de*), but there is a controversy about the meaning of *zhi*. See Zheng Kai, *Between Virtue and Propriety: The History of Thought of the Pre-Qin Period* (SDX Joint Publishing, 2009).

21 See Chen Mengjia, *Survey of Yin Ruins Oracle Inscriptions* (Zhonghua Book Company, 1988).

22 Chen Lai, *Ancient Religion and Ethics: Origin of Confucianism* (SDX Joint Publishing, 1996), p. 106.

23 See Chen Mengjia, *Survey of Yin Ruins Oracle Inscriptions.* This does not mean that Yin people have no faith in the Supreme Deity, but it only means that in Yin people's life there is no direct relation between a sacrifice system and a faith system.

24 Chen Lai, *Ancient Religion and Ethics*, p. 301. Chen Lai pays more attention to the cultural meaning of "five teaching principles" and place it on a par with the Judeo-Christian Ten Commandments.

25 This means that virtue is the "collective property" of a tribe. The saying "same name has similar virtue, and different names have different virtues" reflects the parallelism between a virtue and a tribe. A common idea introduced by Western research holds that the original connotation of virtue is "totem," shared by all members of the clan and then owned by the clan leader or even the king evolved by the status of the clan leader. The meaning of this idea lies in its emphasis on virtue as "collective property," regardless of whether the proper understanding of the concept of totem is appropriate or not.

26 As is well known, Wang Guowei paid particular attention to the historical meaning of the political revolution carried on by the Zhou people against the Yin dynasty, and he stressed the innovative way of thinking of the Zhou people, claiming that "as for every Chinese cultural and political revolutionary change, nothing was more intense than the one during the Zhou and Yin dynasties." Chen Mengjia

criticized Wang Guowei's standpoint, because he ignored the fact that the Zhou people somehow followed the Yin dynasty's social structure. For Wang Guowei's statement, see "On the System of Zhou and Yin Dynasties," in *Collected Essays of Wang Guowei*, Book 10, Vol. 2 (Zhonghua Book Company, 1959), p. 451. For Chen Mengjia's critical point of view, see Chen Mengjia, *Survey of Yin Ruins Oracle Inscriptions*, p. 629 et seq.

27 Hou Wailu, *General History of Chinese Thought*, Book 1 (People's Publishing, 1957), p. 92.

28 Chen Lai, *Ancient Religion and Ethics*, p. 304.

29 For example, the *Book of Songs* reports an entire story that can be said to be a representative example:

> Successors tread in the steps [of their predecessors] in our Zhou. For generations there had been wise kings; The three sovereigns were in Heaven; And King [Wu] was their worthy successor in his capital. King [Wu] was their worthy successor in his capital, Rousing himself to seek for the hereditary virtue, Always striving to accord with the will [of Heaven]; And thus he secured the confidence due to a king. He secured the confidence due to a king, And became a pattern of all below him. Ever thinking how to be filial, his filial mind was the model [which he supplied]. Men loved him, the One man, And responded [to his example] with a docile virtue. Ever thinking how to be filial, he brilliantly continued the doings [of his fathers]. Brilliantly! and his posterity, Continuing to walk in the steps of their forefathers, For myriads of years, Will receive the blessing of Heaven. They will receive the blessing of Heaven, And from the four quarters [of the kingdom] will felicitations come to them. For myriads of years, Will there not be their helpers?
>
> (Quoted from the *Book of Songs*, "The Major Odes. Decade of Wen Wang. Xia Wu," in James Legge [trans.], *The Chinese Classics: With a Translation, Critical and Exegetical Notes, Prolegomena, and Copious Indexes. Confucian Analects, the Great Learning, and the Doctrine of the Mean*, 5 vols. [Trübner, 1861–1872])

30 For example, in the "Heavenly Question" chapter of the *Poetry of the South*, there are two sayings: "Wang Hai inherited the virtue of Wang Ji" and "Wang Heng inherited the virtue of Wang Ji." The meaning is that the descendants (Wang Hai and Wang Heng) inherited the crown of the ancestor (Wang Ji), i.e., they inherited his virtue.

31 A possibly forced explanation but not a pointless opinion is the one expressed by Wang Shenxing, who says that

> the essence of virtue is still filial piety, including filial content, such as Zhou people's filial support and sacrifices for ancestors can be considered as filial conduct. But reverence shown to the Supreme Deity and for Heaven can be considered as virtue: its essence is the way of filial piety to Heaven. In the ideology of Zhou people, the filial respect towards parents and ancestors belongs to filial piety, and the filial reverence to Heaven is virtue. So, it is said that showing reverence to Heaven or showing reverence to virtue means that "virtue" is a substitute expression for the filial attitude towards Heaven.
>
> (See Wang Shenxing, "On the Essence of the Western Zhou Dynasty's Filial Values," *Journal of Humanities*, 1991 [2], pp. 70–76)

32 For an exhaustive discussion on the origin of virtue, see Zheng Kai, *Between Virtue and Propriety*.

33 The connection between the origin of virtue and the séance has been pointed out by Chi Zhongzhong and Guo Moruo, while Li Zehou clearly discussed the connection between the origin of virtue and shamanic practice. See Zheng Kai, *Between Virtue and Propriety*, pp. 59 and 11.

34 Chi Zhongzhong and Guo Moruo actually relate the exegetical explanation of "to be virtuous, is to obtain" to the connection between the origin of virtue and the séance.

35 In this regard, an idea worth mentioning is the interpretation of virtue according to "charisma" in the early religion. For example, Johnson thinks that virtue implies the connotations of authority, property and magic power. See Zheng Kai, *Between Virtue and Propriety*, p. 9.

36 Based on his analysis of the related literature and commentary (such as Qu Tongzu's interpretation that "those with high virtue have profound influence, while those with low virtue have little influence" in the *Guliang Commentary on Spring and Autumn Annals*), Zheng Kai concludes that virtue is closely related to the rank of nobility, to the official position and the official's salary. See Zheng Kai, *Between Virtue and Propriety*, p. 71.

37 It is a common belief that the notion of people is given great importance in the Zhou people's thought. Guo Moruo considered the character *min* (people) in the *Great Yu Tripod* as "those with rude eyes, holding a thorn, with the characteristic signs of slaves," so he interpreted *min* as "slaves." Wang Depei confirmed and developed Guo Moruo's standpoint, and he pointed out that the form of the character *min* is the corrected form of *cong mu*, implying that the correct way to write the character *min* is not related to the saying quoted by Guo, but is consistent with "what is watched from above," thus is connected with the Zhou idea of the people "watched by Heaven." So, Heaven is above, and the people are below, and what Heaven is watching is the people. This interpretation is completely consistent with the concept found in the *Book of Documents*, that "Heaven loves the people," "Heaven sympathizes with the people. What the people desire, Heaven will be found to give effect to," "Heaven sees what my people see; Heaven hears what my people hear." From my perspective, what should be paid more attention is that, if we admit that the evolution from the character *zhi* in the oracle inscriptions is the initial form of the character *de* (virtue), and *min* (people) is the form from *zhi* 直 to *zhi* 置, then there is a relation between the origin of the *de* and *min* characters. Thus, one plausible explanation for the origin of the word "virtue" could be that, if people are what is watched from Heaven, then virtue is looking up at, trusting and following Heaven. That is to say, virtue and people together shaped the bond between men and Heaven from different directions: the former stresses men's reverence and the faith to Heaven, the latter highlights the concern and the requirements shown by Heaven towards men. On the Zhou interpretation of the concept of *min*, see Wang Depei, "Notes on Liji, vol. 1," *Journal of Tianjin Normal University*, 1997 (4), pp. 71–77. In addition, see Ba Xinsheng, *Research on Ethics of the Western Zhou Dynasty* (Tianjin Classics, 1997), p. 22 et seq. He interprets "virtue" in oracle inscriptions as "people acting with reverence and obedience towards the spiritual beings' will."

38 We can also find some evidence about the relationship between the talent and the religious context. The word "*tiancai*" (having an inborn talent) indicates that the

origin of talent can be ascribed to Heaven. If Heaven endows people with some talent to achieve some mission (so-called "putting into practice an individual gift endowed by Heaven"), we could say we have given a general interpretation of "talent" in the religious context. This also means that virtue, to a certain extent, includes talent, or we can say that talent might be a concept separated from virtue. This standpoint can be proved by some literature evidence: for example, when it discusses the *dao*, the *Doctrine of the Mean* states that "great virtue will receive the mandate": "Heaven develops each thing according to its preparation. Thus, Heaven nourishes the growing sprout, and throws down the leaning tree." Another example is in the *Mengzi*, when Mencius uses the idea of talent to explain the value of those who are capable and virtuous: when King Xuan of Qi inquires of Mencius about how to recognize those with talent and those without talent ("How can I recognize those without talent and give them up?"), Mencius answers that he should "promote to office men of talent and send those without talent away" (*Mengzi* IB.14). On another occasion, he also said: "Those who keep the Mean, train up those who do not, and those who have abilities, train up those who have not, and hence men rejoice in having fathers and elder brothers who are possessed of virtue and talent. If they who keep the Mean spurn those who do not, and they who have abilities spurn those who have not, then the space between them—those so gifted and the ungifted—will not admit an inch" (*Mengzi* IVB.35). A typical example is when Mencius tries to explain the goodness of human nature using the idea of talent:

> From the feelings proper to it, it is constituted for the practice of what is good. This is what I mean in saying that nature is good. If men do what is not good, the blame cannot be imputed to their natural powers. [...] Men differ from one another in regard to them—some as much again as others, some five times as much, and some to an incalculable amount—it is because they cannot carry out fully their natural powers.
>
> In good years the children of the people are most of them good, while in bad years the most of them abandon themselves to evil. It is not owing to any difference of their natural powers conferred by Heaven that they are thus different. The abandonment is owing to the circumstances through which they allow their minds to be ensnared and drowned in evil.
>
> (*Mengzi* VIIA.6)

39 If some difference should be considered, the most obvious one is that, for the Zhou people, virtue is some unique ability endowed by Heaven on individuals who deserve to be granted that mandate, while for Mencius, human nature is the peculiar feature endowed by Heaven on each individual receiving his fate, i.e., the most valuable aspect of a human being.

3 Is the Confucian doctrine of benevolence a moralistic doctrine?

Although the Zhou people's spiritual world laid a significant foundation for the formation of early Confucianism's fundamental thought, the thought of Confucius, the founder of Confucianism, is the real symbol of the emergence of Confucianism. So, for those who take moralism as a preconception and for a long time have been used to look at Confucianism through the lens of moralism, it is a more significant choice to explain Confucius' doctrine of benevolence as a moralistic doctrine, in order to bring the fundamental spiritual aim of Confucianism back to moralism. They believe that the essential connotation of Confucius' benevolence is fundamentally "the pure, self-conscious and voluntary altruistic tendency." Benevolence is either interpreted as an innate moral emotion, like sympathy and pity, on the basis of the theory of compassion (*ceyin zhi xin*, 恻隐之心) or explained through resonating and universal love not reaching the principle of Heaven and further regarded as the cosmological essence pervading all things on Earth and Heaven. Regardless of the different explanations, the ultimate aim is to bring the interpretation back to moralism. If we believe what Nietzsche said, "All noble moralities generate from extraordinary self-affirmation,"[1] and if we keep in mind Confucius' instruction of "Learning for the sake of one's self," we cannot but show our doubts about this moralistic interpretation and be aware that it could be a sign of the bad habit of modern morality expressed by the moralistic trend.

There is little argument about summarizing Confucius' thought as a doctrine of benevolence. For Confucius, who dedicated his life to forming his thought and passing it on to future generations, his theory of benevolence is, without any doubt, of the greatest significance and an innovation based on inheriting the spiritual legacy of the Zhou people. Furthermore, it has become the most important and almost iconic idea of the tradition of education initiated by Confucius and named after Confucianism. However, there is still a certain difficulty in achieving a clear understanding of Confucius' benevolence. The first reason is that Confucius is not a philosopher who engaged in theoretical debates but a man who put into practice what he was always concerned about, including virtue cultivation, teaching, moving from place to place following the principle of righteousness and seeking self-improvement.

From *Lunyu* and some literature related to his words and deeds, we can see his random answers to questions on different topics and in different contexts instead of his precise definition of benevolence.

One quite concise lesson of Confucius about benevolence is "the benevolent person loves others." As stated in *Lunyu*, "Fan Chi asked about benevolence. The Master said, 'It is to love all men.'"[2] This statement is simple and clear but easily misunderstood. In order to achieve a deep understanding of the spiritual implication of "the benevolent person loves others," we need a further inquiry and analysis. The issue of "loving others" necessarily involves three elements, including who loves, the ability to love and who is loved. First, "the benevolent person loves others" is effective for those with the ability to love. We need to possess the ability to love to "be" someone who can love, and who is loved can actually "be" who is loved when he has been loved. Clearly, the ability to love is the most important of these three elements. On this basis, if we connect the instruction of "benevolence depends on oneself"[3] and "I wish to be virtuous, and lo! virtue is at hand"[4] and other teachings of Confucius, we will realize that even though Confucius did not give a specific explanation of benevolence from the perspective of human nature, he believed that everyone possesses the ability to love. As for the issue of whether benevolence is an endowed ability for all, Confucius did not provide a clear answer.

Furthermore, a crucial problem lies in whether the benevolence in Confucius' instruction "the benevolent person loves others" means the universal love among human beings or refers to a special relationship between who loves and who is loved. Another problem related to this involves whether the acts of benevolence are directed at some special groups or all humankind and even all things in the universe. When we attentively consider the relationship between who loves and who is loved, we can notice the most representative trait of the spiritual nature of Confucius' doctrine of benevolence. Although Confucius' benevolence could be expanded to all humankind and even all things in the universe, it does not refer to the universal love between human beings. Instead, it refers to a differentiated love based on the special relationship between who loves and who is loved. In other words, the benevolence is differentiated but can be extended to all.

To fully understand this differentiated benevolence, it is necessary to introduce the important role of human relations in Confucianism. In the tradition of education initiated by Confucius and named after Confucianism, filial piety is always the first practical content when teachers educate disciples on how to develop appropriate behaviors and cultivate benevolence and morality, and the benevolence itself is always related to filial piety. As Confucius said:

> Benevolence is the characteristic element of humanity, and the great exercise of it is in loving relatives. Righteousness is the accordance of actions with what is right, and the great exercise of it is in honoring the worthy. The decreasing measures of the love due to relatives, and the steps in the honor due to the worthy, are produced by the principle of propriety.[5]

Moreover, "The essence of being benevolent is to serve one's parents."[6] From the practical instruction of filial piety, we can realize that the actual comprehension of Confucian benevolence is not separated from the context of human relations. If benevolence means that everyone possesses a remarkable ability, human relations are the solid foundation for the practical expression of benevolence. In other words, the benevolence is not an unconditional instruction directed to all without any differentiation, but a virtue based on authentic order among human relations.

As Confucius stated:

> The duties of universal obligation are five and the virtues wherewith they are practiced are three. The duties are those between sovereign and minister, between father and son, between husband and wife, between elder brother and younger, and those belonging to the intercourse of friends. Those five are the duties of universal obligation. Knowledge, benevolence, and courage, these three, are the virtues universally binding. And the means by which they carry the duties into practice is singleness.[7]

This passage clearly expresses the relationship between virtue and human relations. Without virtue, the inner order of human relations (i.e., ethics) is difficult to realize; without this inner order of human relations, the virtue will lose its goal. This is related to the correlation between benevolence and filial piety. In Book I of *Lunyu* we can read the following passage:

> The philosopher You said, "they are few who, being filial and fraternal, are fond of offending against their superiors. There have been none, who, not liking to offend against their superiors, have been fond of stirring up confusion." The superior man bends his attention to what is radical. That being established, all practical courses naturally grow up. Filial piety and fraternal submission!—are they not the root of all benevolent actions?[8]

As one of the disciples of Confucius, what You Ruo said is consistent with Confucius's fundamental idea, where the filial piety and the fraternal duty between fathers and brothers can be regarded as the foundation of being benevolent. Hence, if the focus of "the benevolent person loves others" lies in the manifestation of benevolence, what is more important is that benevolence is love based on the inner order of human relations. We know that Song Confucianism explains benevolence as the principle (*li*) of love, or reads the relationship and difference between benevolence and love according to the relationship and difference between human nature (*xing*) and inner emotions (or passions, *qing*), in order to show the difference between the Confucian benevolence and the Buddhist compassionate love. This is because from the stance of Confucianism, while compassionate love seemingly can be a step forward, it is instead based on a nihilistic premise, as Zhu Xi writes in his

Preface to the Doctrine of the Mean: "Seemingly rational but actually far from the truth."[9]

As for Confucius and Confucianism during the classical age, the importance of human relations initially originates from the experience of real life, for man has always placed himself within interpersonal human relations. One essential point of Confucianism is that "man is by nature an ethical animal."[10] This constitutes the factual basis for the doctrine of differentiated love. In other words, as ethical instruction, differentiated love is deeply rooted in the experience of the real life of human beings. Men live in social groups, and, in the context of real life, there are always some people more valuable to oneself. So, there are indeed differences between close and distant relationships. For instance, although someone might generally possess a clear awareness of showing respect for others, he still will not treat strangers the same as his relatives. The ethical instruction of differentiated love reveals that Confucius' benevolence is not a universal awareness of love towards humankind, so we cannot reconnect it to a kind of abstract humanism.

In Book X of *Lunyu* it is said that "The stable being burned down, when he was at court, on his return he said, 'Has any man been hurt?' He did not ask about the horses."[11] Modern scholars have often interpreted this case of caring about people instead of horses out of context, concluding that Confucianism is essentially a kind of humanism. Obviously, it is a misleading interpretation. Confucius intended to express that he cared more about humans than horses rather than insisting on abstract humanism. Undoubtedly, as with moralism, this abstract humanism belongs to the bad habit of modern morality and there is a close relationship between the two. However, the interpretation that the ethical instruction of differentiated love originates from actual life experience does not mean that the ethical spirit of Confucianism is directly based on kinship, since Confucianism has a more ethical knowledge instead of discussing human relations per se.

Although modern people who attempt to hold a sympathetic understanding of Confucianism are inclined to state that "*Dao* (morality) reflects the real context of human relations", they have to say, on the other hand, that "*Dao* originates from Heaven." It means that the understanding and acknowledgment of Heaven's Mandate are hidden behind the ethical awareness of Confucianism. It is in this aspect that human relations can be directly recognized as ethical family relations, and this is not accidental or irrelevant. There is a saying in the *Book of History*, "talking about *Yi lun*" where *Yi lun* refers to the "cardinal human relationships" or ethical family relations.

In summary, in the context of Confucian thought, human relations (i.e., ethics) are understood and recognized according to the superior principle of Heaven's Mandate. Human relations are in fact the inner principle of Heaven's Mandate. The spiritual purpose of human relations is not restricted to the narrow view of kinship but can also be attributed to the ultimate ethical concern between men and Heaven. If we say that kinship plays a vital role in the original spiritual world of Confucianism, it is because kinship is understood within the concept of Heaven's Mandate.

The concept of Heaven's Mandate is also the reason why differentiated benevolence can be performed and directed to all. Filial piety indeed is the starting point of benevolent integrity, honesty and enlightenment, and it is the foundation of being benevolent. But relatives, friends, neighbors, townsmen, the rich, the poor and even strangers should also be treated with benevolence, i.e., the so-called "treating all with benevolence." Therefore, benevolence could be interpreted as a differentiated love based on human relations and can be continuously expanded and universalized. That is to say, the expression of benevolence is based on authentic moral principles performed among men, and this lays a solid foundation for universalization of love instead of hindering it. It is in this sense that benevolence can be the ethical basis for a community— no matter whether it is a family clan, a society or a nation, or the world—and is politically meaningful. The community proposed by Confucianism is the ethical community grounded on benevolence as a core idea, and this ethical community grounded on benevolence is a community inherently connected to Heaven's Mandate, as the foundation of benevolence is nothing else than the principle of human relations which originates from Heaven. Needless to say, such a community inherently connected to Heaven's Mandate is different from modern nations built on the so-called social contract and established since modern times on the consideration of interest.

Using a kind of language we are familiar with, we can say that benevolence based on the ethical principle of Heaven's Mandate, and thereby stressing differentiated love, is also related to men's understanding of their authenticity. It is the ultimate ethical concern between men and Heaven that defines their authenticity, i.e., men can comprehend their authenticity and answer the question "who am I" only by understanding the principle of Heaven's Mandate. Since understanding of their own authenticity in a sense is equal to comprehension of the principle of Heaven's Mandate, when men understand their authenticity, they realize the meaning of Heaven's Mandate which they possess in their individuality. As far as the experience of real life is concerned, man is by nature an ethical animal: the complex ethical network not only constitutes men's real life but also defines their authenticity. Hence, as differentiated love related to the ethical principle of human relations, benevolence is aimed at achieving human authenticity. As instruction for virtue cultivation, the doctrine of benevolence is the practical instruction for humans to realize their authenticity and complete their existence. As stated in the *Doctrine of the Mean*, "[the superior man] completing himself shows his perfect virtue [benevolence]."[12] Benevolence involves one's authenticity, and authenticity originates from the principle of Heaven's Mandate. Therefore, benevolence is closely related to personal sorrows and joys and directly tends towards human authenticity. Only in the light of this understanding is the idea that benevolence is the actual "learning for the sake of one's self" (*wei ji zhi xue*, 为己之学) advocated by Confucianism. The self is not an empty, disembodied and altruistic moral subject deprived of all particular traits but is a person who seeks vividly and actively puts into practice his moral conduct in a context of individual personality.

Being a kind of love actively performed, benevolence cannot avoid involving others. Hence, we can also analyze the point of "being for others" from the practical instruction of "the benevolent person loves others." Zhang Zai once stated that "loving others with the same affection as loving oneself is being benevolent."[13] This means that benevolence both requires "perfecting oneself" and "perfecting others." But, when we talk about benevolence, we definitely see that it involves others, or that what it involves is based on the ethical principle of human relations and others' authenticity, while others' authenticity is also under the control of the principle of Heaven's Mandate. For one who shows benevolence, the love for others fundamentally is directed towards others' authenticity and the perfection of their personality. The love shown through benevolence is not emotional care imposed on others without considering others' authenticity or even by undermining their authenticity, like sympathy or pity.

In the reality of life experience, those in the ethical network who maintain a close relationship with us, like parents, teachers or friends, or those who keep a distant and not so close relationship with us, like strangers or people living in a neighborhood, all might be among those whom the benevolent person needs to get along with. Hence, if the love shown through benevolence is the principle for human coexistence and the way we maintain close relationships with others, the understanding and acknowledgment of the existence of others' authenticity is enclosed in the ethical teaching of benevolence. The existence of others' authenticity should be fully recognized and perfected regardless of close or distant relationship. We usually explain the meaning of benevolence in terms of the effort of "putting oneself in the place of the other," even regarding this as the core indication of benevolence, aiming to recognize and perfect the existence of others' authenticity entailed in benevolence. In one conversation aimed at settling Zi Gong's doubts, Confucius stated: "Now the man of perfect virtue, wishing to be established himself, seeks also to establish others; wishing to be enlarged himself, he seeks also to enlarge others."[14] When Zhong Gong inquired about benevolence, Confucius said: "What you do not want done to yourself, do not do to others."[15] If the practical instruction "the benevolent person loves others" seems quite simple and may lead to some kind of misunderstanding, comparatively, the expression "putting oneself in the place of the other" could better highlight the spiritual purpose of Confucius' idea of benevolence and, as a result, is regarded as the core principle of his idea of benevolence. This expression seems to indicate more clearly that one who puts into practice the virtue of benevolence actively provides that love based on human relations to those closely related and extends that kind of love to people in general. Using Mencius' words, "putting oneself in the place of the other" implies treat with the reverence due to age the elders in your own family, so that the elders in the families of others shall be similarly treated; treat with the kindness due to youth the young in your own family, so that the young in the families of others shall be similarly treated.[16]

It needs to be pointed out that, because our and others' authenticity is the same, these can both be attributed to the principle of Heaven's Mandate. So, the understanding of "putting oneself in the place of the other" should also be based on this principle. In other words, "putting oneself in the place of the other" means realizing the value of extending Heaven's Mandate granted to oneself to Heaven's Mandate given to others. Therefore, "putting oneself in the place of the other" or "the benevolent person loving others" should not be interpreted as epitomizing the moralistic idea which centers on suffering and enjoyment.

In terms of "treating others" and related to the "good" desired by humans, the instruction written in *Lunyu* stating that "the superior man seeks to perfect the admirable qualities of men, and does not seek to perfect their bad qualities"[17] is a better interpretation of benevolence, for its nature lies in the difference between "good and bad" rather than "good and evil." The altruism contained within benevolence leads to a possible reductive interpretation of benevolence as moralism: by excluding the source of the ethical principle of Heaven's Mandate and considering benevolence as empathic love, we can obtain benevolence's reductive moralistic interpretation.

In the current cultural situation, the essential connotation of moralism always returns to a human will or an emotion: for example, pure and universal goodwill, sympathy and pity to vulnerable people, widespread kindness, sense of charity or general benevolence for all existing beings without difference, expanding to animals, to all lives and even to what is lifeless. Since it is an improper reductive interpretation to understand benevolence as moralism, what is the difference between benevolence and moralistic goodwill and moralistic sympathy? As for this point, we can provide further analysis and interpretation, starting from the following aspects. First, although both benevolence and moralistic goodwill or sympathy entail care for others, their intentions are totally different. Moralistic goodwill or sympathy is caused by the difficulty relating to a vulnerable situation, while benevolence is for a particular person. That is, as a general will or emotion regardless of the objects imposed, moralism focuses on others' miserable situation, while benevolence, based on the differentiated love of human ethical relations, varies according to its different objects. We can see this difference not only reflected in the degree of manifestation, but also in those means through which it reveals itself.

The degree of manifestation and the means connected to love for a father, a mother, a brother and a sister are different from those of love for teachers and friends, and even from those for compatriots: the difference related to means originates from the relation between who loves and who is loved.

Generally speaking, moralism is an emotional concern for one who is vulnerable or shows some weakness, while benevolence is a principle connected to the relationship between our and others' authenticity, "a particular love for a particular person" actively starting from ourselves. Moreover, the main difference between benevolence and moralistic goodwill or sympathy is that the latter considers oneself and others with a nihilistic attitude. The spiritual aim of moralism includes pure voluntary altruism. In this spiritual framework, because they are pure moral subjects, both the self and others are endowed with the esteem and nobility of personality. In such cases, both the self and others are potentially regarded as the vulnerable or weak part, ignoring the human ethical relation inherent to our and others' authenticity. So, moralism considers others with a nihilistic attitude, and nihilism is its spiritual essence. However, benevolence in Confucianism does not belong to formalistic ethics or sympathy ethics, because benevolence is precisely based on the premise of the ethical principle related to the importance of our and others' authenticity. Benevolence is neither "a pure altruistic emotion" nor "a pure altruistic will." Rather than being empty subjects of a sort of formalistic ethics, or fanatics ready for sharing others' sorrow at times for the sake of morality, "the people who show benevolence" are those pursuing moral conduct according to a unique personality and a clear understanding of their authentic existence. Furthermore, despite its altruistic feature, benevolence is, first of all, the ability of self-realization and self-perfection. The reason why the benevolent person loves others is based on the reality of life experience and how he can integrate some particular people into his comprehension of living a good life. Hence, the idea of benevolence cannot be explained according to Xu Fuguan's statement that benevolence is an "unlimited and unconditional duty towards others." People who are benevolent always "first seek for it starting from themselves" and so, desiring a good life starting from themselves, they care about others. That is, benevolent people first love themselves, and benevolence as a virtue first includes self-love and then love for others. However, the love of the benevolent person for others does not aim at taking advantage of others. Instead, he loves others because they are "what they are," just as he loves himself for "what he is." In other words, the love of the benevolent person focuses on moral conduct, and is centered on moral virtue; it is self-love and love for others. Besides, the benevolent person loves others, and by cultivating the virtue of benevolence, he makes himself loveable, then receives love from others. But the compassionate concern advocated by moralism does not originate from a comprehension of a good life, nor does it show a concern for others for "what they are." Fundamentally, this sympathetic love is not self-love for "what we are," nor does is love others for "what they are."

Finally, if the fundamental spirit of moralism lies in nihilism, then moralism contains the anthropological premise that man is a hedonistic animal. Or we can say, moralism lowers the existence of humankind to the level of an animal's feeling of enjoyment and suffering and radically regards the human being as a kind of animal avoiding pain and desiring pleasure. On the contrary, the idea of benevolence maintained by Confucius affirms the role of human beings on the high level of Heaven's Mandate, indicating another anthropological premise instead, i.e., the human being is an ethical animal by nature. From the inner essence of the idea of benevolence, we can see that the anthropological premise enclosed in moralism is quite irreverent and disrespectful of pure and noble human nature: this is a recognizable symptom of modern nihilism.

Notes

1 Friedrich Nietzsche, *On the Genealogy of Morals and Ecce Homo*, trans. by Walter Kaufmann and Reginald J. Hollingdale (Random House, 1967), First Essay, Section 10, p. 36.
2 *Lunyu* XII.22. All translations from *Lunyu* and *Zhongyong* are from James Legge (trans.), *The Chinese Classics: With a Translation, Critical and Exegetical Notes, Prolegomena, and Copious Indexes. Confucian Analects, the Great Learning, and the Doctrine of the Mean*, Vol. 1 (Selbstverlag, 1861), unless otherwise indicated.
3 *Lunyu*, XII.1, translator's note.
4 *Lunyu*, VII.30.
5 *Zhongyong* 20.
6 *Mengzi* IVA.27, translator's note.
7 *Zhongyong* 20 (Legge's translation modified).
8 *Lunyu* I.2.
9 Zhu Xi, *The Collected Four Books* (Zhonghua Book Company, 2012), p. 15, translator's note. This evaluation is suitable for the instruction of love that takes nihilism as its premise. In the current cultural situation, it includes both the charity advocated by secular humanism and the *agape* promoted by Christianity: the essence of both is moralism.
10 "Ethical" here means according to the "principle of human relations."
11 *Lunyu* X.12.
12 *Zhongyong* 26 (Legge's translation modified).
13 Zhang Zai, *Collected Works of Zhang Zai* (Zhonghua Book Company, 1978).
14 *Lunyu* VI.30.
15 *Lunyu* XV.24.
16 *Mengzi* IA.7.
17 *Lunyu* XII.16.

4 Is Mencius' theory of goodness of human nature a moral metaphysics?

Through the moralistic interpretation of Confucius' idea of benevolence and the thought of the Zhou people, moralists depict the outline of Confucian moralism. However, moralists are not satisfied with this. In their opinion, it is Mencius' theory of goodness of human nature that makes Confucian moralism clear and evident. Thus, moralism that seeks morality for the sake of morality is the fundamental spiritual aim of Confucianism, and on this basis, they can better understand the nature of the Confucian spirit.

Mencius' thought plays a vital role in the history of Confucianism, especially after the Tang dynasty. As we all know, Han Yu explicitly included Mencius in Confucian orthodoxy and maintained that Confucian orthodoxy had no successor after Mencius, which supports the concept of Confucian orthodoxy in the Song dynasty. By listing the *Mencius* as one of the Four Books, Zhu Xi placed Mencius' thought among the Classics. More interestingly, although Song-Ming Neo-Confucianism had a close relationship with Mencius' ideas, Mencius' thought has also been a crucial classic work used to criticize Song-Ming Neo-Confucianism, and indeed, the most significant resource in this respect has been Dai Zhen's *Literal Meaning of the Mencius*. In the history of Confucianism, the main contribution of Mencius' thought is the theory of cultivating the inner *qi* (*yang qi*) and especially the theory of the goodness of human nature. Mencius inherited Zi Si's idea that "what Heaven has conferred is called nature," and he discovers "what the former Sages didn't find," putting forward the theory of the goodness of human nature, that is, nature (*xing*) as the heart-mind (*xin*), and laying the foundation for the Neo-Confucian philosophy of Learning of the Heart-and-Mind (*xinxue*).

Moralists, of course, look directly at Mencius' theory of the goodness of human nature and the theory of four moral sprouts closely related to it under the moralistic perspective. According to them, Mencius' theory of goodness of human nature is the typical expression of the spirit of Confucian moralism. This is because Mencius' theory of goodness of human nature is consistent with the idea of compassion inherent in the theory of four moral sprouts, as with moralists' substantial understanding of morality, that is, purely voluntary altruism. Undoubtedly, the moralistic understanding of Mencius' theory of goodness of human nature is still a mainstream view shared and recognized by most scholars, although different opinions exist regarding its specific interpretation. Likewise, no one would argue against the fact that, among the modern New-Confucian scholars, Mou Zongsan and his "moral metaphysics" have exerted to the utmost the moralistic understanding of Mencius' theory of goodness of human nature.[1]

From the perspective of the evolution and development of Confucianism, Mou Zongsan's thought has an apparent affinity with the Song and Ming dynasties' Learning of the Heart-and-Mind. However, even in the tradition of Confucian moral education, the meaning of Mou Zongsan's thought cannot be understood only from a thinking affinity or according to the tradition of *yili* ("meaning and pattern") interpretation. Social conditions play a role in the emergence of any new thought. Even though the role may be peripheral, the social conditions under which a thought emerges are significant for the understanding of its meaning. Mou Zongsan lived in the era when modern Western culture penetrated China and gradually occupied the mainstream. Especially after the May Fourth New Culture Movement in 1919, the tradition of Confucian moral education suffered an unprecedented attack. Through a quite common association, China's military and political failure was directly linked to and consequently seen as derived from the tradition of Confucian moral education. As the Enlightenment trend of checking everything through rationality became popular, ways of thinking also underwent a significant change. The Western paradigm has always displayed its rationality, and thus settled in the field of Chinese ideology in the name of rationality, gradually becoming the dominant mode for ideological inquiry and knowledge production. Consequently, the study of Confucian Classics inevitably declined and was replaced by Chinese philosophy in a modern sense. Chinese philosophy in a modern sense refers to traditional Chinese philosophy crossed with modern Western philosophy. Mou Zongsan's thought falls in this category. Therefore, Mou Zongsan developed his own thought not only in a comparative dialogue with Western philosophy, but also under the guidance of the Western rational paradigm. If we take his substantial spiritual tendency into account, then we can say more explicitly that Mou's thought is a creative interpretation of traditional Confucianism in comparison with Western philosophy and in comparison with Kantianism; also, it is a kind of revaluation of the spirit of traditional Chinese thought, especially the spirit of traditional Confucian education, under modern conditions and guided by rationality.

Mou Zongsan interpreted the status of morality in the tradition of Confucian education on the basis of Western philosophy's metaphysics. He claimed that Mencius' concept of "nature" is the metaphysical noumenon, namely the "substance of nature" (*xingti*). If Mencius advocated the theory of goodness of human nature, that means that the substance of nature is a pure moral noumenon. At the same time, regarding the heart-mind as nature, as for the idea of compassion and the theory of the four moral sprouts, Mou Zongsan believed that this similarity was entirely consistent with the theory of goodness of human nature. That is, compassion is just another expression of the pure moral substance of nature: the substance of the heart-mind (*xinti*) is the same as the substance of nature (*xingti*), referring to a pure moral noumenon. Since the substance of the heart-mind mainly tends to denote a moral subject, or is a term referring to a moral subject, the semantic sliding from the substance of the heart-mind to the substance of nature shows that the moral subject is the moral noumenon. Obviously, to some extent, this carries out the idea that "only entity can serve as the subject" held by Western metaphysics. On the other hand, the substance of the heart-mind is proposed to imply the authentic reality of the moral noumenon: that is, the moral noumenon is not in a distant place or a pure theoretical hypothesis, but is present directly in the heart, Thus it becomes a direct and ultimate moral foundation:

> "Sense of compassion" is the transcendental basis of "moral practice" and the stable foundation of moral idealism. Without compassion, we cannot describe moral practice or even practice. "Practice" is man's duty, not a thing's duty. Any human practice cannot be carried out without the general state of compassion. If without this state, although practice can still be performed, it cannot be considered as practice: it can be only considered as an active manifestation of an object, and it will not have any value or meaning in human society.[2]

In other words, Mou Zongsan directly understood Mencius' theory of goodness of human nature in terms of a sense of compassion. Based on the integration of the heart-mind and nature philosophical interpretations, Mou Zongsan proposed that Mencius' theory of goodness of human nature and theory of the four moral sprouts actually constitute a moral metaphysics structurally different from Western metaphysics, and generally defined as moral idealism. His view became a core point of modern Neo-Confucianism. In their opinion, moral metaphysics, or moral idealism, is the essence of Chinese cultural spirit. Mou Zongsan understood the connotation of "morality" and "goodness" according to a modern moral way; that is to say, closely linked with purely voluntary altruism. Therefore, moral idealism or moral metaphysics proposed by Mou Zongsan through the interpretation of Mencius and other thinkers' thought, has become, in the philosophical morphology of moral realism, the highest representation of this moralistic interpretation of Confucian educational spirit in modern times.

As we have already mentioned, Mou Zongsan's metaphysical interpretation of Mencius's theory of heart-mind/nature is made in contrast with Western philosophy, especially in contrast with Kantian philosophy. Thus, Mou Zongsan paid special attention to the differences among the moral metaphysics in his interpretation, Kant's "metaphysics of morals" and the ideas of several Western moral philosophers. In this regard, in some critical academic contributions, Li Minghui made a very detailed and exhaustive analysis.[3] He pointed out that the structure of the moral subject is the key to understanding the difference between Mou Zongsan's moral metaphysics and

Kant's Western moral philosophy. Speaking of Mencius' thought, the crucial point lies in how to understand the meaning of Mencius' four moral sprouts and sense of compassion, that is, the heart-mind/nature. Generally speaking, according to Mou Zongsan, Mencius' four moral sprouts and sense of compassion cannot be interpreted as moral feelings from the perspective of an emotivism theorist, such as Shaftesbury, or as in Kant's late thought. Instead, they can be understood as an ontological feeling, similar to the connotation proposed by phenomenologists like Max Scheler. Essentially, the sense of compassion is a transcendent essential heart-mind. This idea has put an ontological or existential mark on the sense of compassion and has put forward an idea of what may be called ontological moralism as a fundamental paradigm to understand Confucianism.

This ontological or existential moralistic idea stresses the importance of the theory of the four moral sprouts and even sees it as more crucial than the theory of goodness of human nature. It reveals that only by grasping the meanings of compassion, shamefulness, reverence and righteousness related to those four moral sprouts can we understand the meaning of the theory of goodness of human nature. However, even in the direct relationship between the heart-mind and nature, the latter is more important than the former. Therefore, in order to understand and disclose the core meaning of the theory of the four moral sprouts, it is more relevant to comprehend Mencius' theory of goodness of human nature, rather than to focus on the meaning of the heart-mind/nature and the relationship between them.

Mencius undoubtedly proposed the theory of the four moral sprouts, i.e., the theory of heart-mind/nature, to clarify the theory of goodness of human nature:

> Gongduzi said, "The philosopher Gaozi says, 'Man's nature is neither good nor bad.' Some say, 'Man's nature may be made to practice good, and it may be made to practice evil, and accordingly, under Wen and Wu, the people loved what was good, while under Yu and Li, they loved what was cruel.' Some say, 'The nature of some is good, and the nature of others is bad. Hence it was that under such a sovereign as Yao there yet appeared Xiang; that with such a father as Gu Sou there yet appeared Shun; and that with Zhou for their sovereign, and the son of their elder brother besides, there were found Qi, the viscount of Wei, and the prince Bi Gan.' And now you say, 'The nature is good.' Then are all those wrong?" Mencius said, "From the feelings proper to it, it is constituted for the practice of what is good. This is what I mean in saying that the nature is good. If men do what is not good, the blame cannot be imputed to their natural powers. The feeling of commiseration belongs to all men; so does that of shame and dislike; and that of reverence and respect; and that of approving and disapproving. The feeling of commiseration implies the principle of benevolence; that of shame and dislike, the principle of righteousness; that of reverence and respect, the principle

of propriety; and that of approving and disapproving, the principle of knowledge. Benevolence, righteousness, propriety, and knowledge are not infused into us from without. We are certainly furnished with them. And a different view simply owes to want of reflection. Hence it is said, 'Seek and you will find them. Neglect and you will lose them.' Men differ from one another in regard to them—some as much again as others, some five times as much, and some to an incalculable amount—it is because they cannot carry out fully their natural powers. It is written in the Book of Poetry, 'Heaven in producing mankind, gave them their various faculties and relations with their specific laws. These are the invariable rules of nature for all to hold, and all love this admirable virtue.' Confucius said, 'The maker of this ode knew indeed the principle of our nature!' We may thus see that every faculty and relation must have its law, and since there are invariable rules for all to hold, they consequently love this admirable virtue."

Clearly, when Gongduzi asked Mencius whether human nature is good or not, Mencius explained to him his idea of the goodness of human nature and added a further explanation about the four moral sprouts. According to moralists' point of view, Mencius' theory of goodness of human nature is obviously and directly connected with the theory of the four moral sprouts, especially with the sense of compassion. The sense of compassion is often understood as a sympathetic feeling which implies purely voluntary altruistic tendency. Instead, goodness related to the theory of goodness of human nature is understood, within the context of modern morality, as a value judgment from the perspective of the beneficiary: goodness refers to being "good" to others. Thus, the sense of compassion and the theory of goodness of human nature are regarded as the same. However, this moralistic interpretation is indeed a misconception, demeaning, or even disrespectful of Mencius' thought. Mencius spoke highly of human nature. Thus, stating that Mencius only advocates a moralistic spiritual interest is entirely wrong. The subversion of the meaning of "goodness" related to the theory of goodness of human nature and the theory of the four moral sprouts (especially the meaning of sense of compassion) helped to define this moralistic interpretation of Mencius' thought.

In the quoted passage, Gongduzi stated his different view from Mencius' theory of goodness of human nature, according to three points: the first, human nature is neither good nor bad; the second, human nature may practice good, and it may practice evil; the third, some people's are good, and some others' are bad. In this context, we speak about the relative relation between goodness and cruelty. Moreover, Emperor Wen of the Zhou dynasty, Emperor Wu of the Zhou dynasty, Yao, Shun, Weizi Qi and the prince Bi Gan are regarded as examples of goodness, while Emperor You of the Zhou dynasty, Emperor Li of the Zhou dynasty, Xiang, Gu Sou and Emperor Zhou of the Shang dynasty are regarded as examples of evil. Here "goodness" refers to good behavior, focusing on the appraisal of good or evil conduct. On this point, Mencius claimed that,

> From the feelings proper to it, it is constituted for the practice of what is good. This is what I mean in saying that the nature is good. If men do what is not good, the blame cannot be imputed to their natural powers.

In Mencius' opinion, the evil conduct of You, Li, Xiang, Zhou and others doesn't mean that human nature is evil, but the good conduct of Yao, Shun, Wen, Wu and others represents the goodness of human nature. In other words, the goodness or evil of human nature and of human behaviors are not the same. If the evaluation of human behaviors is on a different degree, and the goodness of human nature is related to the evaluation of endowed ability (to be good), Mencius positively affirmed that men can do good actions. Thus, Mencius' theory of goodness of human nature confirms that men have the ability to do good actions. So, the statement "men are born with goodness" means that if men follow their human nature and follow their innate ability, their behavior will be authentically good. If we insist on a specific premise, i.e., the a priori ontological nature of goodness, we will find that the substance of goodness of human nature is a coincidence. In other words, based on our understanding of the substance of goodness, we can see that human nature is coincidentally good. However, if man's behaviors derive from his innate ability, goodness is an appraisal of human behavior, and, furthermore, goodness is directly connected with the intrinsic quality of human behavior. It is then quite clear that it is not that human nature happens to be good that makes human behavior good, but that men give positive confirmation in themselves that their nature is good, and this makes human behavior good. We can see that Mencius' theory of goodness of human nature is an affirmation of our human nature and innate ability, nothing else.

It is essential to clarify this point. For example, in the debate over human nature between Mencius and the philosopher Gaozi, Gaozi compared the willow to human nature and cups and bowls to benevolence and righteousness. And Mencius replied,

> Can you, leaving untouched the nature of the willow, make with it cups and bowls? You must do violence and injury to the willow, before you can make cups and bowls with it. If you must do violence and injury to the willow in order to make cups and bowls with it, on your principles you must, in the same way, do violence and injury to humanity in order to fashion from it benevolence and righteousness! Your words, alas! would certainly lead all men on to reckon benevolence and righteousness to be calamities.
>
> (*Mengzi* XIB.1)

This shows that following the nature of the willow or forcing it is the boundary line setting the significant value. Equally, following the nature of the willow or forcing it is also the dividing line between goodness and evil. With his theory of goodness of human nature, Mencius states that human nature determines man's goodness, instead of the appraisal of the goodness of human nature according to the a priori ontological nature of goodness.

In addition, Gaozi compared flowing water to human nature. He said:

> Man's nature is like water whirling round in a corner. Open a passage for it to the east, and it will flow to the east; open a passage for it to the west, and it will flow to the west. Man's nature is indifferent to good and evil, just as the water is indifferent to the east and west.

Mencius replied:

> Water indeed will flow indifferently to the east or west, but will it flow indifferently up or down? The tendency of man's nature to good is like the tendency of water to flow downwards. There are none but have this tendency to good, just as all water flows downwards. Now by striking water and causing it to leap up, you may make it go over your forehead, and, by damming and leading it you may force it up a hill—but are such movements according to the nature of water? It is the force applied which causes them. When men are made to do what is not good, their nature is dealt with in this way.
>
> *(Mengzi* XIB.2)

The tendency of water to flow downwards belongs to its nature, while leaping up, going over the forehead or flowing up a hill are results derived from the force applied which causes them. Here, taking water as exemplifying the human being, the force applied is seen as the evil, while the tendency of water to flow downwards because of its inner nature is seen as the goodness. The boundary between goodness and evil is the difference between the tendency related to inner nature and the force applied. In other words, the meaning of goodness of human nature is that goodness is determined by the inner nature, rather than the inner nature being appraised by goodness.

Based on the above analysis, we can definitely conclude that in Mencius' theory of goodness of human nature, the appraisal of the goodness of human nature is not based on the idea of an a priori ontological nature of goodness (especially the concept of goodness as understood by moralists), but it is a direct affirmation of human nature: the idea of goodness is grounded in human nature. Goodness is appraised by human nature, not vice versa. The meaning of goodness cannot be understood as an essentially altruistic spirit in a moralistic sense. The tendency to flow downwards is an affirmation and a value definition. Therefore, the goodness of human nature doesn't refer to the innate altruistic or sympathetic tendency claimed by the moralists, but is an affirmation of the human being's extraordinary part, a "beautification" of human being itself. In other words, it refers to the perfection and aspiration of human nature.[4]

What also needs to be pointed out is that in the current understanding of Mencius' theory of goodness of human nature there is not only a common misunderstanding of what "goodness" is, but also a misunderstanding of what "human nature" is. A very famous debate between the philosopher Gaozi and Mencius is frequently quoted, but unfortunately, it has not been understood correctly. It reads as follows:

> The philosopher Gaozi said, "Life is what we call nature!" Mencius asked him, "Do you say that by nature you mean life, just as you say that white is white?" "Yes, I do." Mencius added, "Is the whiteness of a white feather like that of white snow, and the whiteness of white snow like that of white jade?" Gaozi again said "Yes." "Very well," pursued Mencius. "Is the nature of a dog like the nature of an ox, and the nature of an ox like the nature of a man?"

Mou Zongsan, Xu Fuguan and other scholars believe that Mencius did not agree with Gaozi's statement on "life is what we call nature", because "life is what we call nature" is actually the nature that a man was born with, and it refers only to the nature of desire or our temperament, not the nature that is endowed by Heaven. Here there is a severe misunderstanding. In fact, "life is what we call nature" is only an etymological or semantic interpretation, and it is what Mencius and the philosopher Gaozi acknowledged in a previous stage of the debate.

Mencius' refutation of Gaozi is not directed at refuting the statement that "life is what we call nature," but instead directs him towards a correct understanding, reassessing his erroneous position by reduction to absurdity, and not understanding "life is what is meant by nature" in the same way as "white is white." In fact, nature and white are two different concepts. Edmund Husserl points out that a conceptual hierarchy can be formed according to different degrees of abstraction, from the lowest to the highest. For example, we can infer the abstract concept of "whiteness" from a white feather, white snow and white jade, or understand by abstraction the concept of "color" from red, white and blue, and, moreover, we can recognize the sensory quality from all the various colors. We can then infer by abstraction the essence from the sensory quality, the subject from the essence. However, in this sequential hierarchy, two different concepts are included. One is a general concept, such as white. It is limited to the field of the object, i.e., the collection of all the white things belongs to the object field of "white color." The other one is the formal concept, such as "essence": this is not limited to a particular object field but denotes the function of that interconnection. The conceptual abstraction starts from generalization and ends with formalization. For example, inferring by abstraction from the color to the sensory quality still falls into the general concept scope, but inferring by abstraction from sensory quality to essence belongs to the formal concept scope. The difference between formal concept and general concept lies in that the latter can be directly understood through the object field it is limited to, while the former cannot be understood from a relevant object field and can only be regarded as a pure demonstrative indication of interconnection.[5]

According to Husserl's analysis of the difference between the abstraction method related to those two concepts, we can properly understand the correct connotation in the debate between Mencius and the philosopher Gaozi. Mencius does not mean that starting from "life is what we call nature" we will assume a wrong conclusion, that is, "the nature of a dog is like the nature of an ox, and the nature of an ox is like the nature of a man," but that the interpretation of "life is what we call nature" cannot be equivalent to that of "white is white." This is because "white" is limited to an object field, that is, inferred by abstraction from specific objects, including a white feather, white snow and white jade, while nature is different. Nature is not, like whiteness, limited to an object field: that is, a common and shared "nature" cannot be inferred by abstraction from the nature of dog, cattle and man. It is clear that Gaozi misunderstands the formal concept of "nature" as a general concept like "white," which is a first crucial misunderstanding in Gaozi's interpretation of "nature." Mencius does not explain "nature" as a general concept with substantive content, but as a formal concept denoting interconnection. In other words, "nature" does not refer to something substantive, but it is an indication of a relation or interconnection. For example, "nature" in the statement "life is what we call nature" is used to indicate the relationship between life and who grants life. Dogs are born dogs, cattle are cattle, men are men, so the relationship between the dog's and Heaven's life, and what it is born with, is called the dog's nature. Likewise, the relationship between cattle and Heaven's life, and what it is born with, is called cattle's nature, and the relationship between man and Heaven's life, and what he is born with, is known as "human nature." Although there is the same notion of "nature": the natures of the dog, cattle, and human are different, because among dogs, cattle and human beings there is a vast difference. Mencius wrote, "That whereby man differs from the lower animals is but small. The mass of people cast it away, while superior men preserve it" (*Mengzi* IVB.47).

It is essential to point out that man and animals are different not because man is a moral animal with a sympathetic sense of compassion, as moralists assert, but because man possesses his fate, the Mandate granted by Heaven (*tianming*). It is through human nature that the nature of dogs, cattle and other things can exist. Among all things, man is the most essential and spiritual. The existence of all things (being what they should be) is achieved and completed by human beings. In this sense, human nature is an essential part of the existence of all things, and an essential part of the statement "things find their nature and life under *The Great Change of Heaven*." The reason why man possesses the Mandate granted by Heaven is that man is born to accomplish the noble mission of making all things to be complete in their existence as what they should be. Man is born to perform his mission according to the process of creation and transformation of the universe. Only when we understand human nature according to the Mandate of Heaven, and not in the sense of moralism, can we see the worth of the human being. It is worth noting that making everything complete in its existence as it should be is different from the preservation of all things. The latter is the viewpoint of ontological moralism.

As we all know, Mencius' theory of goodness of human nature originates from the idea advocated by Zisi that "what Heaven has conferred is called 'nature'. An accordance with this nature is called the path of duty; the regulation of this path is called instruction." We can say Mencius has very deep understanding of the concept of "what is granted by Heaven" (*tianming*). For example, Mencius said in a very terse and positive tone:

> There is an appointment for everything. A man should receive submissively what may be correctly ascribed thereto. Therefore, he who has the true idea of what is Heaven's appointment will not stand beneath a precipitous wall. Death sustained in the discharge of one's duties may correctly be ascribed to the appointment of Heaven. Death under handcuffs and fetters cannot correctly be so ascribed.
>
> (*Mengzi* VIIA.2)

Therefore, in Mencius' opinion, human nature is the relationship between man and Heaven. The doctrine related to following and complying with Heaven directly contains the understanding of human nature. In other words, men have the ability to understand, expand and achieve the Mandate granted by Heaven, which is the direct source of human nature. Namely, human nature is nothing else but the ability to understand, expand and achieve this. Therefore, in this noble spiritual context, Mencius' theory of goodness of human nature refers indeed to the understanding and affirmation of Heaven. Or, in front of Heaven's Mandate, men comprehend their own excellence and nobility. Here there is no substantial moral principle, but the recognition of one's potential. Goodness doesn't focus on concern for others, but on the ultimate concern for oneself. Mencius said:

> There is a way to the attainment of sincerity in one's self. If a man does not understand what is good, he will not attain sincerity in himself. Therefore, sincerity is the way of Heaven. To think how to be sincere is the way of man.
>
> (*Mengzi* IVA.12)

The attainment of sincerity in one's self implies the real understanding of oneself, so the way to the attainment of sincerity in one's self lies in "understanding what is good" and is based on the genuine concern between man himself and Heaven. In this sense, goodness is not desirable because of others, but for oneself, as the perfection we realize for ourselves as self-fulfillment, self-realization and self-improvement.

If we analyze it from the perspective of religious psychology, the affirmation of our human extraordinary part in front of Heaven makes the relationship between man and Heaven no longer like the relationship between debtor and creditor. Nietzsche revealed that in the spiritual world of Christianity, the relationship between man and God is a relationship between debtor and creditor. This also becomes the true origin of the Christian notion of original sin, because it triggers the self-denial of man in the face of God:

> A man *is willing* to confess his unpayable guilt, and is blamed for his guilt; he *is willing* to admit that none of his guilts can be compensated by any punishment; he *is willing* to poison the foundation of things with guilt and punishment, in order to stop him from walking out of the maze of "fixed ideas"; he is willing to build the ideal of "sacred god" to confirm that he is worthless.[6]

While the Christian notion of original sin comes from the deranged will connected to the keen awareness of being in debt in front of God, Mencius' theory of goodness of human nature is just the opposite. Mencius confirms the value of human beings in front of Heaven and lays a solid foundation for the perfectibility of all things, which is the authentic meaning of his statement "All things are already complete in us. There is no greater delight than to be conscious of sincerity on self-examination" (*Mengzi* VIIA.4). This means that the relationship between man and Heaven is not the relationship between debtor and creditor, but the relationship between bailee and bailor. In this relationship, men are born noble and pure and carry out their mission to perfection, i.e., the mission assigned by Heaven. If we connect Mencius' theory of goodness of human nature with the Zhou people's respect and reverence for morality, the connection carried forward is evident. The difference between the two lies in that the Zhou people still consider "virtue" (*de*, 德) as the talent of a minority, while Mencius maintains that everyone is the carrier of his fate, the Mandate of Heaven, and this is the exact connotation when he says that "everyone can be Yao and Shun," and "the Sage and we are the same in kind."

The goodness of human nature is a value definition, referring to the extraordinary affirmation of man's excellence and nobility, and the perfect character of human nature. Thus, the crucial point is how men can grasp it. Men understand that they receive and hold the Mandate of Heaven and comprehend their nobility. This is the process through which the value setting of the goodness of human nature is defined:

> Mencius said, "For the mouth to desire sweet tastes, the eye to desire beautiful colours, the ear to desire pleasant sounds, the nose to desire fragrant odours, and the four limbs to desire ease and rest—these things

are natural. But there is the appointment of Heaven in connection with them, and the superior man does not say in his pursuit of them, 'It is my nature.' The exercise of love between father and son, the observance of righteousness between sovereign and minister, the rules of ceremony between guest and host, the display of knowledge in recognising the talented, and the fulfilling the heavenly course by the sage—these are the appointment of Heaven. But there is an adaptation of our nature for them. The superior man does not say, in reference to them, 'It is the appointment of Heaven.'"

(*Mengzi* VIIB.70)

"Nature" and "Heaven" are what we called "establishing of Heaven's Mandate (*li ming*, 立命) and preserving the inner nature (*cun xing*, 存性)," that is, the process of recognizing the correct appointment granted by Heaven as the cultivation of human nature in our heart-minds, and it is the definition of the value of goodness of human nature. If men fail to understand in which way they are guided by the Mandate of Heaven, they will not understand the inherent perfection of human nature. Thus, the crucial point related to the goodness of human nature is men's ability to comprehend the Mandate of Heaven. Mencius introduced his idea of "preserving the heart-mind" (*cun xin*, 存心) from this perspective:

Mencius said, "That whereby the superior man is distinguished from other men is what he preserves in his heart—namely, benevolence and propriety."

(*Mengzi* IVB.56)

Gongduzi said, "All are equally men, but some are great men, and some are little men—how is this?" Mencius replied, "Those who follow that part of themselves which is great are great men; those who follow that part which is little are little men." Gongduzi pursued, "All are equally men, but some follow that part of themselves which is great, and some follow that part which is little—how is this?" Mencius answered, "The senses of hearing and seeing do not think, and are obscured by external things. When one thing comes into contact with another, as a matter of course it leads it away. To the mind belongs the office of thinking. By thinking, it gets the right view of things; by neglecting to think, it fails to do this. These—the senses and the mind—are what Heaven has given to us. Let a man first stand fast in the supremacy of the nobler part of his constitution, and the inferior part will not be able to take it from him. It is simply this which makes the great man."

(*Mengzi* VIA.15)

"The senses of hearing and seeing do not think, while to the mind belongs the office of thinking": here the difference is illustrated from their function.

Compared with the awareness of the ear and the eyes (the sense of hearing and seeing), the heart-mind displays a special awareness (the ability to think). Through the ability to think with the heart-mind, man is able to comprehend "what the Heaven gives to men"; he can "first stand fast in the supremacy of the noble part of his constitution" (*xian li yu qi da*, 先立乎其大), be aware and recognize his noble part and be in accord with it, thus he can be a great and superior man. The reason why great men are different from ordinary people is that they can understand what Heaven commands them to do. In other words, they can fully comprehend the noble human nature, the relationship between human beings and the Mandate of Heaven and men's nobility and dignity in front of the Mandate of Heaven. In this sense, we can say that the knowledge from ears and eyes is that of hearing and seeing, while the knowledge of the heart-mind is that of moral virtue. The knowledge of hearing and seeing comes from things, while the knowledge of moral virtue attains Heaven. Therefore, the perfect goodness of human nature can only be achieved thanks to the ability to think of the heart-mind. If one's heart-mind is "ensnared and drowned" (*xian ni qi xin*, 陷溺其心) for some reason, the brilliance of the perfect goodness of human nature cannot be revealed. In this sense, "preserving the heart-mind" and "the goodness of human nature" are the same. "Preserving the heart-mind" is not only the epistemological basis for the goodness of human nature, but also the condition of its existence.

This is probably the only correct way to understand Mencius' idea of heart-mind/nature and disclose the meaning of the theory of the four moral sprouts. Mencius once used the story "a child is about to fall into the well" as an example to explain that everyone has the sense of compassion, i.e., "not bearing to see the sufferings of others," in order to conclude that all men have the four moral sprouts in their heart-mind:

> Mencius said, "All men have a mind which cannot bear to see the sufferings of others. When I say that all men have a mind which cannot bear to see the sufferings of others, my meaning may be illustrated thus: even now-a-days, if men suddenly see a child about to fall into a well, they will without exception experience a feeling of alarm and distress. They will feel so, not as a ground on which they may gain the favor of the child's parents, nor as a ground on which they may seek the praise of their neighbors and friends, nor from a dislike to the reputation of having been unmoved by such a thing. From this case we may perceive that the feeling of compassion is essential to man, that the feeling of shame and dislike is essential to man, that the feeling of modesty and complaisance is essential to man, and that the feeling of approving and disapproving is essential to man. The feeling of compassion is the principle of benevolence. The feeling of shame and dislike is the principle of righteousness. The feeling of modesty and complaisance is the principle of propriety. The feeling of approving and disapproving is the principle of knowledge. Men have these four principles just as they have their four limbs. When

men, having these four principles, yet say of themselves that they cannot develop them, they play the thief with themselves, and he who says of his prince that he cannot develop them plays the thief with his prince. Since all men have these four principles in themselves, let them know to give them all their development and completion, and the issue will be like that of fire which has begun to burn, or that of a spring which has begun to find vent. Let them have their complete development, and they will suffice to love and protect all within the four seas. Let them be denied that development, and they will not suffice for a man to serve his parents with."

(Mengzi IIA.6)

The moralistic interpretation of Mencius' theory of the four moral sprouts focuses on the understanding of compassion. More specifically, the heart-mind which possesses the sense of compassion is the heart-mind "not bearing to see the sufferings of others." Therefore, those who pledge a moralistic position can directly regard "children" as the personification of "others," and see the sense of compassion as the sympathetic emotion related to others' diseases or sufferings, a spontaneous feeling that comes from the depth of one's heart and a feeling of caring for others. Hence, the first problem we must confront with is: according to Mencius, is the sense of compassion felt when "a child is about to fall into the well" a sympathetic feeling for others' misfortune? Alternatively, is it an empathy triggered by others' plight?

As stated above, the heart-mind possessing the sense of compassion is a short version for what we can call a heart-mind which feels apprehensive by fright and compassion. Xu Shen said in his *Shuowen Jiezi* that "Fear (*chu*, 怵) refers to being afraid, to fear (*kong*, 恐)", "To be vigilant (*ti*, 惕) refers to being respectful (*jing*, 敬)", "To feel anguish (*ce*, 惻) refers to pain (*tong*, 痛)" and "Solicitous (*yin*, 愍) refers to pain (*tong*, 痛)".[7] Zhu Xi mentioned in *Collected Commentary on the Mengzi* that "fear makes man pale. *Ce* and *Yin* refers to deep sadness." Therefore, the heart-mind which feels apprehensive by fright and compassion includes the feelings of fear, respect and pain. Undoubtedly, the heart-mind which feels apprehensive by fright and compassion includes a feeling of immediate concern for oneself. Since the heart-mind which feels apprehensive by fright and compassion, in terms of the heart-mind not bearing to see the sufferings of others, involves care for others, at the same time it involves concern for oneself. Thus, with the heart-mind which feels apprehensive by fright and compassion, in what sense is this a kind of empathy? According to a logical manifestation of empathy, when the witness confronts the situation that a child is about to fall into the well, he will think that he might fall into the same situation. Thus, the feeling of fear, respect and pain appears, and the empathic feeling for the child in distress occurs. In other words, it is the self-concern of the witness that makes that incident (that a child is about to fall into a well) deeply touch his heart, which is pure and bears no other reason. He will feel this way, not that he may gain the favor of the child's parents, nor that he may seek the praise of the neighbors and friends, nor from a dislike of the reputation of having been unmoved by such a thing. In this sense, the "child" is a personification of oneself, rather than merely of others. Because the suffering of "a child" is understood as that of oneself, a man will have the feeling of fear and pain when seeing a child that is about to fall into a well, and it is the heart-mind which feels apprehensive by fright and compassion.

However, if we explain the heart-mind which feels apprehensive by fright and compassion as the manifestation of empathy from the point of view of empirical psychology, we may overlook a crucial problem behind Mencius' argumentation related to it. In Mencius' thought, how and in what sense should a man treat a child? Closely related to this problem, in what sense should one understand the suffering of a child? If we analyze this problem from a more general perspective, it can be converted into the following question: how and in what sense should a man treat oneself? How should a man treat others? Ultimately, how should a man treat people? Also, how should man understand people's sufferings?

In the spiritual tradition of Confucianism, what is similar to the sufferings of the child who is about to fall into the well should be attributed to fate (*ming*, 命). When Zixia helped Sima Niu relieve his concern he said, "Death and life have their determined appointment; riches and honors depend upon Heaven" (*Lunyu* XII.5). Confucius lamented over his fate many times. For example, when Bo Niu, one of his disciples, fell ill, he said, "One's death is determined by fate" (*Lunyu* VI.10). Besides, Confucius considered that the rise and fall of the *dao* were decided by fate: "If my principles are to advance, it is so ordered. If they are to fall to the ground, it is so ordered" (*Lunyu* XIV.36). Mencius developed a deep understanding of "fate" or "destiny" (*ming*, 命):

> That which is done without man's doing is from Heaven. That which happens without man's causing is from the ordinance of Heaven.
>
> (*Mengzi* VA.6)

> Mencius said, "There is an appointment for everything. A man should receive submissively what may be correctly ascribed thereto. Therefore, he who has the true idea of what is Heaven's appointment will not stand beneath a precipitous wall. Death sustained in the discharge of one's duties may correctly be ascribed to the appointment of Heaven. Death under handcuffs and fetters cannot correctly be so ascribed."
>
> (*Mengzi* VIIA.2)

According to Mencius' opinion, all of this is the ordinance of Heaven "which happens without man's causing," but there is still the difference between the right appointment of Heaven and what does not correctly belong to the appointment of Heaven. Therefore, for men, the key point for human beings is to be able to see this difference, accepting and following the correct path. We know that Mencius associates the appointment of Heaven with human nature. That is, men recognize and follow the appointment of Heaven as their human nature, as stated before in terms of "establishing of Heaven's Mandate (*li ming*, 立命) and preserving the inner nature (*cun xing*, 存性)." Moreover, this is how the superior men can be different from ordinary people, by "preserving the heart-mind." Therefore, "carrying on our conduct according to Heaven (*li ming*, 立命) by nurturing and preserving our nature (*cun xing*, 存性)" actually means to distinguish between right and wrong. That is, to comprehend the perfection of the right appointment by Heaven correctly necessarily means to understand the "ugliness" of the incorrect. In other words, "one who knows Heaven" understands that the "appointment of Heaven" of "the death sustained in the discharge of one's duties" must contain the understanding of what is not "appointed by Heaven." Only in this way may he practice his life-long caution of "not standing beneath a precipitous wall." On the contrary, what belongs to a non-appointment of Heaven can produce a tremendous force, which can prompt people to pay more attention and cherish the goodness of life.

It is clear that, in the example of Mencius' heart-mind which feels apprehensive by fright and compassion, the situation that a child falls into a well is not only an experience of misfortune or bad luck, in other words, this situation cannot only be understood as pure suffering because misfortune, but it is a misfortune in the sense of non-appointment of Heaven. In this way, the sense of compassion arising in the heart-mind when we see a child falling into a well should be understood as the emotion felt when we are in front of a situation related to non-appointment of Heaven. Moreover, the feeling of fear and misery concerning something wrong or bad (related to a non-appointment of Heaven) makes man cherish what is appointed by Heaven. In the example of a child who is about to fall into a well, Mencius' concern is the misfortune the child suffers, rather than the fact that this situation may be attributed or not to Heaven. We also should assume that the reason why a man feels fear and pain when faced with a child who is about to fall into a well is that he relies on the fate granted by Heaven and affirms himself and others in an extraordinary way, thus affirming his human nature and the perfection of this nature. In this sense, regardless of his personification of others or oneself, the child is what embodies, substantially, the appointment of Heaven. If the heart-mind which feels compassion shifts to a positive emotion from fear and pain, it will not be sympathy but cherishing of the self and others: fundamentally, to cherish the fate appointed by Heaven and the goodness of human nature itself. Therefore, from a negative point of view, the correct connotation of the heart-mind which feels compassion is a fearful, painful or regretful feeling related to what is not appointed by Heaven and which arises when we understand the appointment of Heaven, while from a positive point of view, it is a feeling of respect and gratitude produced by the goodness of human nature when recognizing the fate decided by Heaven.

Here, someone who advocates a moralistic interpretation might say that, since it is correct to explain the heart-mind which feels apprehensive by fright and compassion as cherishing the goodness of human nature, such an explanation shows no contradiction with the moralistic interpretation of the heart-mind which feels apprehensive by fright and compassion. This is because a moralistic emotion of compassion and sympathy can be analyzed starting from a feeling of cherishing and regret. This assertion clearly demonstrates the main reason for the moralistic interpretation of the theory of four moral sprouts but neglects a more significant problem, that is, consistently preserving a differentiated ethical order based on the assumption that the heart-mind of compassion is the sprout of benevolence. In other words, if the theory of four moral sprouts within the framework of Confucian thought mainly focuses on the motivational factors related to the ethical agency of human beings, it is even more important that, in this framework, the comprehensive understanding of ethical agency cannot be achieved only by a motivational factor. Taking benevolence as an example, it is enough to understand the real meaning of benevolence only from the motivational factor of the mental palpitation caused by fear and compassion. The other side of the meaning of benevolence, actually a more fundamental side, is the recognition of ethical principle, that is, as Confucius said, "benevolence is that man loves his parents" (*Rites—The Doctrine of the Mean*); Mencius said, "The richest fruit of benevolence is this: the service of one's parents" (*Mengzi* VIIA.27). Only the heart-mind with a sense of compassion as a motivational factor, combined with the ethical principle as a purpose factor, can produce a comprehensive understanding of benevolence. In other words, understanding benevolence only from the perspective of heart-mind with a sense of compassion is unilateral.

An even more severe unilateral moralistic explanation of the theory of four moral sprouts reveals that, usually, we discuss only the heart-mind with a sense of compassion as the sprout of benevolence, forgetting to pay attention to the other three moral sprouts. Or, although we discuss the four moral sprouts in our argumentation, we reductively understand these four sprouts as one. In fact, if we avoid simplifying and reducing the four moral sprouts of benevolence, righteousness, rites and intelligence to one (benevolence), and understand their differences and correlations, we could escape from the moralistic interpretation of them. Bernard Williams once revealed that the moral concept expressed by Kant aimed to maintain such an equal notion in terms of its theoretical purpose: everyone has a moral ability to practice. Two essential theoretical measures should be taken to ensure this purpose is implemented: first, the ability to practice morality must fall entirely on the will of the one who implements this ability, so that it can be free from any other factors and can be open to anyone. Second, it must also be recognized that morality has a supreme dignity and importance, that is, moral value is recognized as the highest value, otherwise it does not make much sense even that this equality is recognized.[8] If we are able to avoid the reduction of the four moral sprouts into one and we can grasp instead their meaning on the basis of their differences and correlations, even though the heart-mind with a sense of compassion as the sprout of benevolence is regarded as a sympathetic feeling of pure goodness, we cannot accept the moralistic interpretation of the four moral sprouts. This is because the moral sprout of benevolence, as one of the four sprouts, based on that interpretation cannot include the meaning of the other three moral sprouts. Thus, with this restriction, it does not have the highest value. In fact, the sense of shame, the sense of respect and reverence and the sense of approving and disapproving are related to the comprehension of Heaven's Mandate and human nature. In short, if man cannot truly understand Heaven's Mandate and the goodness of human nature, he cannot correctly possess the senses of commiseration, respect and reverence and approving and disapproving. More generally, the heart-mind which includes these four moral sprouts is a true comprehension of Heaven's Mandate and the goodness of human nature. The statement "what belong by his nature to the superior man are benevolence, righteousness, propriety and knowledge" does not say that men are born with the moral feeling to show compassion towards others, but it says that men are born with the ability to understand Heaven's Mandate and the goodness of human nature, and with the ability to cultivate their nature according to Heaven. As has been explained earlier, since men are endowed with Heaven's favor and have the innate ability to show the value of what has been bestowed, this innate ability can be understood as the inherent ability to reveal the value of oneself. Benevolence, righteousness, rites and intelligence are the virtues of self-realization, the virtues that men need to live a good life, and how men display the innate favor given by Heaven. Therefore, according to Mencius' theory of "exerting the heart-mind," "heart-mind," "nature" and "Heaven" form a meaningful cycle:

> Mencius said, "He who has exhausted all of his mental constitution knows his nature. Knowing his nature, he knows Heaven. To preserve one's mental constitution and nourish one's nature is the way to serve Heaven. When neither a premature death nor long life causes a man any double-mindedness, he waits in the cultivation of his personal character for whatever issue. This is the way in which he establishes his Heaven-ordained being."
>
> (*Mengzi* VIIA.1)

The "exhaustion of all his mental constitution" is actually "serving Heaven," but Heaven's appointment never stops. It means that men placing themselves in the fate decided by Heaven can have a lifelong prospect. In this way, "the exhaustion of one's mental constitution" is impossible to achieve at once, and it does not represent a manifestation of a mysterious moral noumenon but is an art to achieving morality, requiring practical wisdom, self-cultivation and continuous learning. In this sense, Mencius regards the sense of compassion, the sense of shame, the sense of respect and reverence and the sense of approving and disapproving as the beginning of benevolence, righteousness, rites and intelligence. Discussing the achievement of virtue, Mencius says,

Of all seeds the best are the five kinds of grain, yet if they be not ripe, they are not equal to the *ti* or the *bai*. So, the value of benevolence depends entirely on its being brought to maturity.

(*Mengzi* VIA.19)

It means that "the heart-mind of compassion" as the sprout of benevolence is like a pure and beautiful seed. If a man wants to be a benevolent person, he needs to cultivate it. If the gift of benevolence comes from Heaven, from the innate favor generated by Heaven, the achievement of benevolence is an art needing man's effort and fortune. From a cosmological point of view, the core thought of Confucianism can be summarized as follows: all changes in the universe rely on human culture, but human ability relies on what is given by Heaven.

To sum up, as the moralistic interpretation of the theory of the goodness of human nature is wrong, the moralistic interpretation of the four moral sprouts is also not right. The heart-mind possessing the four moral sprouts does not refer to care for others, but directly refers to the ultimate concern for oneself, to the feelings one experiences when one is in distress. The theory of four moral sprouts focuses on the awareness and acknowledgment of Heaven's Mandate, and on the distinction between Heaven's appointment and the non-appointment of Heaven—that is, the goodness of human nature and the affirmation of man's extraordinary position. Moreover, on this is based the functional difference between man as a human being, and men and animals. Men can think because they have the heart-mind. Men can comprehend, carry out and achieve the fate granted by Heaven. From the standpoint of Confucianism, when human beings affirm themselves, accepting favor within the religious perspective, then the goodness of human nature is not harmed and human dignity is not insulted.

Notes

1 For the Chinese translation of "metaphysics," Mou Zongsan in his article used *xing shang xue*, but here the author uses the term *xing er shang xue* as a standard.
2 Mou Zongsan, *Moral Idealism* (Student Book Store, 1992), p. 24.
3 See Li Minghui, *Confucianism and Kant* (Linking Publishing, 1990).
4 In the *Shuowen Jiezi* it is said that "beauty and goodness have the same meaning." Mencius in *Mengzi* VIIB.71: "A man who commands our liking and he whose goodness is part of himself." Mencius held different attitudes towards "nourishing men by his excellence" and "subduing men by his excellence." Mencius said:

> Never has he who would by his excellence subdue men been able to subdue them. Let a prince seek by his excellence to nourish men, and he will be able to subdue the whole kingdom. It is impossible that any one should become ruler of the people to whom they have not yielded the subjection of the heart.
>
> (*Mengzi* IVB.44)

5 See Edmund Husserl, *General Introduction to a Pure Phenomenology*, trans. by Li Youzheng (Commercial Press, 1992), p. 66 et seq. Zhang Xianglong once stressed the importance of the thought for Martin Heidegger. See Zhang Xianglong, *Martin Heidegger Biography* (Hebei People's Press, 1998), p. 96 et seq.

6 Friedrich Nietzsche, *On the Genealogy of Morals and Ecce Homo*, trans. by Walter Kaufmann and Reginald J. Hollingdale (Random House, 1967), Second Essay, Section 22, p. 93.

7 According to Duan Yucai's *Annotation on the Shuowen Jiezi*, 隐 (*yin*) is a phonetic loan character of 㥯.

8 On this point, see Williams' analysis in Bernard Williams, *Moral Luck* (Cambridge University Press, 1981).

Part II

The appropriation of autonomy

Abstract: Part II criticizes the legalization caused by Mou Zongsan's misappropriation of Kant's concept of autonomy when interpreting Confucianism, which ignores entirely that Confucian tradition is actually a kind of virtue ethics.

5 The spirit of Confucian ethics and autonomous morality

"Autonomous morality" is a core concept in Mou Zongsan's understanding and interpretation of Confucian thought. In one of his most important works, *The Substance of Mind and the Substance of Nature*, he writes:

> Thus, we see that the whole Confucian lineage from the pre-Qin to the Song-Ming all identifies mind and nature as the same thing, maintaining that the self-governance, autonomy, self-determination, and self-guidance of the mind is *li* (理, "principle"). [...] This is the true, morally creative metaphysical reality of our nature. [...] It is on the basis of its self-governance, autonomy, self-determination, and self-guidance that we can speak of an "ought," and it alone can support and preserve the moral "ought." This is genuinely idealist autonomous morality or "oriented ethics."[1]

As long and complex as the history of Confucian thought is, that did not stop Mou from expressing a definitive judgment on the spirit of Confucian ethics. The idea of "autonomous morality" became Mou's paradigm for understanding and explaining the Confucian ethos, and it runs through nearly every chapter and every section of *The Substance of Mind and the Substance of Nature*. Of course, one point needs to be clearly emphasized. Even though Mou's thought is most closely connected to and consistent with Song-Ming Neo-Confucianism, especially with Wang Yangming's thought, as is so often evident in his work *The Substance of Mind and the Substance of Nature* which mainly discusses the spiritual and intellectual world of Song-Ming Neo-Confucianism, Mou's fundamental opinion about the spirit of Confucian ethics comes from his understanding and interpretation of Mencius' thought. It would not be too much to say that this is the key to Mou's renarration and reconstruction of what he called the "universe of cultural consciousness."[2] And Mou puts it even more directly and plainly in his *Treatise on the Summum Bonum*, where he says: "Mencius' basic doctrine is precisely autonomous morality. Appearing for the first time two thousand years ago, it was very incisive and outstanding: this was Mencius' extraordinary wisdom, though the language and way of thinking were different from Kant's."[3] What is especially noteworthy here is Mou's phrase "appearing for the first time." The upshot is, Mou believes that in the unified comparison of Chinese and European culture, the genealogical starting point of autonomous morality should be traced back to Mencius instead of Kant.

Straightforwardly, Mou is playing an academic game of "China had it first." The tread of this argument can be divided into three steps: first is the discovery of the importance of autonomous morality in modern European thought, especially in Kant's; secondly, to look back from Kant's ethics of autonomy to the Chinese intellectual tradition and identify Mencius' and his successors' fundamental doctrine as autonomous morality, thus shaping the spiritual root of Confucian ethical thought in the same way; and finally, to name Mencius as the discoverer of autonomous morality and expound the differences between the Mencian and the Kantian ideas of autonomous morality. Of course, if in any time or any context we could find things of value in our own civilization's ancient tradition which win the esteem of other civilizations, this would be somehow acceptable and perhaps even something to be pleased with. But the crucial problem is that something which appears to be good at certain times or from certain perspectives may not be suitable when placed in a larger traditional or historical context. Thus, it is not only doubtful whether (or in what sense and to what degree) Mencius' thought is reducible to autonomous morality, but it is also questionable whether autonomous morality itself is reasonable.[4]

The connection between autonomy and morality was a significant event in the history of thought of European ethics. The concept of autonomy, developed by Europeans amid the tension between the sacred and the secular, became a hallmark of early modernity. An essential feature of modern European moral philosophy was that the origin of morality does not lie outside of inner humanity: that is to say, morality is grounded in human autonomy, and this has become a very familiar and intelligible point of view for us.[5] Though the emphasis on morality has its origins in the history of European ethical thought, it was Kant who indeed linked them together directly. Kant's naming the autonomy of the will as the highest principle of morality aroused a "Copernican revolution" in practical philosophy.

For Kant, the concepts of autonomy and freedom are closely connected; that is to say, understanding the fundamental meaning of autonomy requires relating it to freedom. Freedom is not an object of intuition and, as rational beings, our thinking is inextricable from categories: so, in order to reflect on "freedom" we need to find the right categories. Since freedom can be taken as the distinguishing characteristic of the will of a rational agent and will is expressed in our behavior and action as a kind of causality, Kant believes that causality is the proper category for the freedom of thought. This point seems easy enough to understand, as we can take the reason for any volitional behavior to be a will capable of free choice. And in this special sort of causality found in the behavior of rational agents, Kant discovered the key to understanding freedom. In other words, in our behavior, i.e., in that special causality connected to the will, there is Kant's idea of practical freedom.[6]

Kant points out that practical freedom has both a negative and a positive sense. In its negative sense, the core implication is that the will of a rational agent is independent from the coercion of impulses of sensibility; therefore, Kant distinguished two different kinds of choice. Sensible impulses possess a pathological sort of coercion, and Kant labeled the choice stimulated by coercive sense impulses of this kind "animal choice" (*arbitrium brutum*), whereas humans' choices are a kind of "free choice" (*arbitrium liberum*) that can be independent from sense impulses, since "in the human being there is a faculty of determining oneself from oneself, independently of necessitation by sensible impulses."[7] However, this negative view of freedom is unfruitful for "insight into its essence,"[8] since, as is obvious, to conceptualize it as "independence of necessitation by sense impulses" is to speak only in terms of some resistance to obstacles. In positive terms, the crucial point of freedom is man's innate "faculty of determining oneself from oneself." This is positive freedom, whose central implication is rational agents' ability to legislate for themselves. It is only in the will's self-legislation that rational agents are positively freed from animal choice and truly master themselves.

The double connotation of freedom of the will matches that of autonomy of the will. As far as the origin of the concept of autonomy is concerned, given in particular the peculiar influence of Christianity on Western history, we should properly define autonomy as referring to independence from any authority (such as a religious or political authority) that is external to oneself and not legislated by oneself.[9] In other words, independence from sense impulses and external authority is the negative implication of the concept of autonomy, and the self-legislation of the will is the positive one. There is another point that we must put in evidence concerning Kant's understanding of the concept of autonomy, namely the concept of law that it entails. As we know, the concept of autonomy is paired with that of heteronomy. Laws exist in nature because natural necessity exists, owing to natural causality. Kant points out that natural causality appears to be a kind of heteronomy since in the activity of natural things (irrational beings) the reason for the production of any effect is not itself. The inferential pattern for this kind of causality is "because A, then B." For example, "because the sun is shining, so the rock is hot." Accordingly, laws also exist in practice because, given the causality of freedom as the basis, there must also be a necessity of freedom. The difference, however, is that the necessity of freedom takes the form of a kind of autonomy because, given what it entails, the behavior demanded by this sort of necessity must be the expression of a free will which is its reason. According to Kant's view, in order for free will to be expressed in active behavior, there must be self-legislation that regulates that action. That is, only self-made law can guarantee that the behavior of a rational agent is the expression of his own free will and his free will is the reason for his action. The inferential model at work in this kind of causality is "because I ought to do this, I can do this." So, for example, "I can be honest because I ought to be honest." This is the famous formula that "ought implies can."[10] Therefore, we can see that Kant's explicit proposition of his concept of freedom is inextricably linked to his introduction of the concept of law under the category of causality. Thus, Kant's concept of freedom contains the concept of law, just as his concept of heteronomy also contains the concept of law. In other words, the concept of law under the category of causality, which is inextricably linked with early modern scientific thought, especially the revolution in physics, is actually the foundation of Kant's concept of freedom. This is the reason that Kant ultimately bound up the freedom and autonomy of the will so closely together with universal moral law.

The fundamental characteristic of morality is autonomy. That is, autonomy of the will must be understood as the highest principle of morality. In this sense, only autonomous morality is possible; there can be no heteronomous morality. In other words, the formulation "autonomous morality" contains a certain redundancy, whereas "heteronomous morality" is as much an oxymoron, like a "square circle." In its negative aspect, freedom is freedom from the domination of an external authority or the needs of sensibility. In its positive aspect, it refers to the self-mastery of the will, to self-legislation. This is Kant's fundamental perspective on morality and autonomy. Mou Zongsan basically inherits the Kantian perspective, even though he interprets Confucian thought by adopting the concept of autonomy, and then, he criticizes Kant's view of autonomy from a Confucian standpoint. There are two extremely important points to note about Mou's judgments regarding the essence of the Confucian ethical spirit: first is that he classifies Confucian ethical thought as moral philosophy (albeit "moral metaphysics") and moreover as "moral philosophy" in the modern Western sense. Second, he believes that autonomous morality is the only correct position and he classifies the spirit of Confucian ethics as autonomous morality. In my opinion, both points are extremely problematic, and mislead our understanding of Confucian ethics, especially early Confucian ethics.

Notes

1 Mou Zongsan, *The Substance of Mind and the Substance of Nature*, Vol. 3 (Shanghai Ancient Books, 1999), p. 97.
2 This is a concept that Mou introduced in his essay "In Memory of Tang Junyi," where he wrote,

> Tang was a giant of the "universe of cultural consciousness." [...] By the "universe of cultural consciousness" I mean something different from just "the cultural scene," for cultural consciousness is different from culture. It is unique to

the Chinese cultural tradition, developed out of rising and falling tides of Xia, Shang, and Zhou culture and passed on through the moral teachings of inner sageliness and outer kingliness of Confucius and Mencius.

(Mou Zongsan, *Moral Idealism* [Student Book Store, 1992], p. 226)

A close connection is apparent between Mou's "universe of cultural consciousness" and his oft-used concept of "cultural life." If "life" here is related mainly to "inner nature" and "universe" to "existence," then according to Mou's line of thinking the universe of cultural consciousness would be built on the basis of cultural life. In other words, the universe of cultural consciousness is a cosmological structural concept of cultural life, a spiritual world made from historical culture. Though Mou speaks of the Xia, Shang and Zhou, and Confucius together with Mencius here, there is no doubt of Mencius' key place in Confucian orthodoxy.

3 Mou Zongsan, *Treatise on the Summum Bonum* (Student Book Store, 1985), Preface.

4 On doubts about the reducibility of Mencian thought to autonomous morality, see the work of Huang Jinxing, Sun Zhenqing and others. Mou's disciple Li Minghui has made a detailed response to these doubts in *Confucianism and Kant* (Linking Publishing, 1990). Among Chinese mainland scholars who addressed this issue, we mention Yang Zebo and Guo Qiyong. However, most observers have kept to Mou's primary line of thinking and confined themselves to criticism or revision of minor details. Doubts about moral autonomy itself come mostly from the virtue ethics trend arising in the Western academic world in the latter half of the twentieth century, most notably from Bernard Williams. See his "Shame and Autonomy" in *Shame and Necessity* (University of California Press, 1993), and "Persons, Character, and Morality" in *Moral Luck* (Cambridge University Press, 1981).

5 On the formation and diffusion of the idea of autonomy in the history of European ethical thought, see Jerome B. Schneewind, *The Invention of Autonomy: A History of Modern Moral Philosophy* (Cambridge University Press, 1997).

6 Here we only discuss practical freedom. For a priori freedom as the basis of practical freedom, and the relation between them, see the discussion in the following chapter.

7 Immanuel Kant, *Critique of Pure Reason*, ed. by Paul Guyer and Allen W. Wood (Cambridge University Press, 1998), A534/B562.

8 Immanuel Kant, *Groundwork of the Metaphysics of Morals*, 4:446, ed. and trans. by Mary Gregor (Cambridge University Press, 1998).

9 The influence of Rousseau's idea of autonomy on Kant is often mentioned. For Rousseau, the public will being based on free self-legislation is the only legitimate source of political authority, which obviously implies the exclusion of any other external authority from legitimacy. Thus, the importance of authority which is independent from external sources and self-legislated for the concept of autonomy in the political sense goes without saying (and this is one reason for the widespread adoption and acceptance of the concept of "autonomy" today). Nevertheless, Rousseau also approaches his portrayal of autonomy in terms of freedom in a moral sense, of independence from sensibility. The interrelationship of moral freedom and autonomy of the will in Rousseau can be seen in Book I, Chap. 8 of *The Social Contract*: "moral freedom alone enables man to be truly master of himself, for the impulse of mere appetite is slavery, while obedience to a self-prescribed law is freedom." See Jean-Jacques Rousseau, *Social Contract and the First and Second Discourses*, ed. by Susan Dunn (Yale University Press, 2002), p. 167.

10 We can say that "ought implies can" is inferred from the analysis of the natural endowment of freedom to man. First of all, by getting through the self-legislation, we can then realize the freedom of will: therefore, "freedom" implies "ought." Secondly, through the ability based on self-determined conduct, that is to say, the ability to submit oneself to "ought" and act, we can accomplish the freedom of will. Thus, if "ought" has to realize the freedom of will correctly, it has to embody "can." In other words, to recognize the freedom of will is the essential feature of man as human being, so it must be recognized that "ought implies can."

6 Mencius on the internality of benevolence and righteousness

As mentioned above, Mou based his claim about the spirit of Confucian ethics on his understanding of Mencius' thought. According to Mou Zongsan, Mencius' theory of the "internality of *ren* and *yi*" suggests that Mencius' thought advocated a kind of autonomous morality. In his *Treatise on the Summum Bonum*, Mou gives a full commentary on *Mencius*' Books VI and VII, in which a significant part concerns Mencius' doctrine of the internality of *ren* and *yi*. Let us first analyze that doctrine in detail and then examine Mou Zongsan's related views.

In the *Mencius*, the discussions on *ren*, *yi*, internality and externality are collected in Book VI, mostly in the following two passages:

> Gaozi said, "The desires for food and sex are our nature. *Ren* is internal; it is not external. *Yi* is external; it is not internal." Mencius asked, "Why do you say that *ren* is internal and *yi* is external?" Gaozi said, "They are elder, and we venerate them. It is not that they are elder because of us. Similarly, that is white, and we treat it as white, according to its being white externally to us. Hence, I say it is external." Mencius replied, "Elderliness is different from whiteness. The whiteness of a horse is not different from the whiteness of a gray-haired person. But, surely, we do not regard the elderliness of an old horse as being not different from the elderliness of an old person. Furthermore, do you say that the one who is elder is displaying *yi*, or the one who venerates him?" Gaozi said, "My younger brother I love; the younger brother of a person from Qin I do not love. I take this as having to do with my own happiness. Hence, I say that it is internal. I venerate an elder from Chu, but I also venerate my own elder. I take this as having to do with the elder's happiness. Hence, I say that it is external." Mencius replied, "Savoring the roast of a person from Qin is not different from savoring my roast. So, it is also thus with objects. Is savoring a roast, then, also external?"

> Meng Jizi asked Gongduzi, "Why do you say that *yi* is internal?" Gongduzi replied, "I act out of my respect; hence I say that it is internal." Meng Jizi asked, "If a fellow villager is older than your eldest brother by a year,

then whom do you respect?" Gongduzi replied, "I respect my brother." Meng Jizi asked, "When you are pouring wine, whom do you serve first?" Gongduzi replied, "I first pour wine for the fellow villager." Meng Jizi concluded, "The one whom you respect is here, but the one whom you venerate is there. Hence, it really is external. It does not come from how you feel internally." Gongduzi was not able to answer. He told Mencius about it. Mencius said, "Next time, ask him, 'Do you show respect to your uncle or your younger brother?' He will say, 'I show respect to my uncle.' Then you say, 'When your younger brother is playing the part of the deceased in the sacrifice, then to whom do you show respect?' He will say, 'I show respect to my younger brother.' Then you say, 'What happened to showing respect to your uncle?' He will say, 'It changes because of the role my younger brother occupies.' Then you also say, 'The reason why my display of respect changes is because it has to do with the role my fellow villager occupies. Ordinary respect is directed toward my brother, but temporary respect is directed toward the fellow villager.'" Meng Jizi, upon hearing all this, said, "Regardless of whether it is your uncle or your younger brother, it is the same respect. So, it really is external. It does not come from how you feel internally." Gongduzi replied, "On a winter day, one drinks hot broth; on a summer day, one drinks cool water. So, are drinking and eating external too?"[1]

As these passages show, Gaozi claims that re*n i*s internal but yi *is* external. In the pre-Qin literary records, we can also find this position in the "Canons: Part II" of the *Mozi* and the "Admonitions" chapter of the *Guanzi*, as well as in the "Six Virtues," "Revering Virtue and Propriety" and "Thicket of Sayings: Part I" unearthed at Guodian. Moreover, we find this position criticized in the "Explanation of the Canons: Part I" in the *Mozi*. From these texts, we can conclude that it was most likely a prevalent and well-established idea at the time, although Gaozi and Mencius presented different perspectives on it. Gaozi upheld his own version of the opinion that *ren* is internal and *yi* is external, whereas Mencius disagreed with it and set forth the reasons for his doubt. And furthermore, it is extremely important to note that it is Mencius' doctrine that "*ren* and *yi* are internal" that draws Gaozi's objection. That is, it is only because Gaozi disagrees with Mencius' doctrine that he challenges him.

We need to clarify, first of all, that despite their divergent opinions and disagreements, Gaozi and Mencius share common beliefs about the actual content of the ethical life. Both acknowledge that, as far as ethical living is concerned, *ren* essentially corresponds to loving one's relatives and *yi* to showing respect to one's elders. Gaozi adduces the example of "loving one's own brother, not the brother of a person from Qin," as the proof that *ren* is internal, and "showing respect both to an elder person from Chu and as well as to one's own elder" as an example of *yi* being external. Mencius undoubtedly admits not just the truth of Gaozi's examples but also their reasonableness, for Mencius himself said, "Treating one's parents as parents is *ren*; venerating one's elders is *yi*" (7A.15), and this alone shows very clearly that Mencius agrees completely with Gaozi about the actual content of *ren* and *yi* in ethical living. That is, these common beliefs about the ethical life are the prerequisites for Mencius' and Gaozi's subsequent disagreements. In fact, we can reasonably guess that these beliefs of theirs about *ren* as loving one's relatives and *yi* as revering one's elders form for them a kind of inherited tradition, and their respective understandings represent discrepant ways of thinking about this tradition. And this is a reminder to us that, as two cardinal virtues of ethical living, *ren* and *yi* are fundamentally different from abstract moral laws, being instead intimately tied to actual ethical living.

Since there are different understandings of exactly what it would mean for *ren* to be "internal" and *yi* "external," we cannot simply declare in vague terms that Mencius accepts or rejects that view without first doing some careful analyses. Certainly, Mencius and Gaozi both affirm the traditional practical faith in *ren* as loving one's relatives and *yi* as revering one's elders, while Mencius opposes Gaozi's opinion that the one is "internal" and the other "external." The Guodian version of the "Six Virtues" gives a unique sort of explanation for the internality of *ren* and externality of *yi*:

> *Ren* is internal; *yi* is external. Rites and music are shared. The internal establishes the father, son, and husband; the external establishes ruler, minister, and wife. [...] In ruling inside the gate, mercy covers up *yi*; in ruling outside the gate, *yi* subdues mercy.[2]

From this context it is apparent that "internal" and "external" here means "inside or outside the gate," namely "the gate of the family." We find almost the same statement in the "Original Fate," the *Rites of the Elder Dai* and the "Four Principles Underlying the Dress of Mourning" in the *Book of Rites*: "In ruling inside the gate, mercy covers up *yi*; in ruling outside the gate, *yi* trumps mercy." Since other texts (such as Book VI of the *Mencius*) do not appear to be calling *ren* and *yi* "internal" and "external" in this familial sense, different interpretations of "internal" and "external" arose. As spatial metaphors, it is not very clear what they refer to. In the "Six Virtues" and "Four Principles Underlying the Dress of Mourning," they are clearly demarcating two kinds of ethical life, with the family as internal and the extended clan, the country and the world as external. In that sense, the internality of *ren* and externality of *yi* means that these two cardinal virtues have a different significance and importance in different ethical contexts. Specifically, in family matters *ren* is primary; in the affairs of society, *yi* must take first place. So, what would Gaozi and Mencius make of this? A reasonable assumption is that, to some degree, neither of them would object. Of course, we must follow this up by clarifying this statement. Gaozi not only explicitly states that *ren* is internal and *yi* external, he also shows by his examples that his own understanding of that doctrine does not conflict with the explanation in the "Six Virtues," "Original Fate" or "Four Principles of Mourning Dress," even though he is not in complete accord with them. For Mencius, if the idea were just not put in terms of "internal" and "external"—if that particular pair of opposing concepts were avoided and attention were just focused exclusively on the intellectual content being expressed—then Mencius might not object.[3]

Another traditional way of delineating "internal" and "external" employs the idea of a "self," such that "internal" and "external" means "inside or outside the bounds of the self." Although this "self" is still not yet clear enough and needs further explanation, we can conclude from the foregoing passages that, at least on its surface, Gaozi's doctrine of the internality of *ren* and externality of *yi* distinguishes internal from external by reference to the boundaries of the "self," and that Mencius' doubts are directed specifically at this claim. And it is this that makes the problem even more complex. Even though Gaozi distinguishes internal and external with reference to the self, his examples are closely connected to the distinction between the intra-familial and extra-familial ethical contexts: this applies both to his example of "loving one's brother rather than the brother of a person from Qin" and also that of "venerating an elder from Chu as well as one's own elder," for obviously "loving one's brother" is intra-familial and "venerating an elder from Chu" is extra-familial. It must be pointed out that "one's own elder" refers to elders outside one's immediate family but inside the clan, so that "venerating one's own elder" is something "outside the gate," and this creates a possibility for confusion. When Gaozi says that "*ren* is within and *yi* without," does he mean inside and outside the bounds of the family gate or of the self? If we look at Gaozi's examples, he seems to be talking about the family gate, but if we look at the concepts used in his explanations, he seems to mean "inside the self" and "outside the self."

Of course, this is a point that we can settle by noticing that although Gaozi's examples consistently use the "family gate" as the line of demarcation between internal and external, in his reasoning he is distinguishing them by reference to the self. That is, the latter interpretation is more appropriate, and we should also notice that distinguishing internal from external by using the self or the family is not an either/or matter. For example, consider the well-known view that, in some sense, "I am my world." Or, in more definite terms, when a person's self-identification is conjoined directly with some boundary or other in his or her ethical life, the two lines of demarcation may end up equivalent. In this instance, if the ethical relationships "inside the gate" of the family constitute the self in the most important sense—that is, if the family forms the nucleus for self-identification—then using the self and using the family gate to distinguish internal from external are in this sense equivalent to one another. And not only can we attribute this view to Gaozi, we can also point out another equally reasonable conclusion: the notion that "*ren* is internal and *yi* external" may have been a deeply and widely held traditional belief, one which may have been variously understood but was intimately connected with the distinction of ethical life into distinct intra-familial and extra-familial contexts, and indeed that this distinction may have served as the practical foundation of that notion. Because Mencius agreed to some extent that *ren* should reign within the family and *yi* without, we can affirm that the focal point of the controversy between him and Gaozi lies elsewhere.

Then, what is their controversy really about? As we know, Mencius and Gaozi's most famous debate involves the question of human nature. The precondition for Mencius' theory that human nature is good is his taking "*ren* and *yi*" as inherent in human nature: "*Ren, yi, li,* and *zhi* are not welded to us externally. We inherently have them."[4] And the preconditions for Gaozi's theory that "human nature is neither good nor not good" are taking "the desires for food and sex [as] our nature" (6A.4) and *ren* and *yi* as *not* inherent in human nature. As Gaozi says, "Human nature is like a willow tree; *yi* is like cups and bowls. To make human nature *ren* and *yi* is like making a willow tree into cups and bowls."[5] From this we can see clearly that their debate about the internality or externality of *ren* and *yi* is subordinate to their debate about human nature. Specifically, Gaozi contends that *ren* is internal and *yi* external in order to oppose Mencius' view that *ren* and *yi* are inherent in human nature, and Mencius' opposition to Gaozi's doctrine of *ren* and *yi* is for the sake of stating his own view that "we inherently have [*ren* and *yi*]." That is, when Gaozi opposes Mencius' doctrine that *ren* and *yi* are given in human nature, he then resorts to the traditional view that "*ren* is internal and *yi* external." This means that the point of the two philosophers' debate about the internality or externality of *ren* and *yi* is whether these are inherent in human nature. This provides us an appropriate starting point to understand this debate.

Let us return to the text: "Gaozi said, The desires for food and sex are our nature. *Ren* is internal; it is not external. *Yi* is external; it is not internal." At first glance, it appears that Gaozi is talking about two problems here, that of human nature and that of the internality or externality of *ren* and *yi*. But why should he put these two problems together? Given the context, we have reason to raise such a question. Drawing on the previous analysis, we can realize that Gaozi's intent here is to separate human nature from *ren* and *yi*. He means to say that *ren* and *yi* are to be distinguished as internal and external and indeed can only be understood in those terms, not in terms of whether they are inherent in human nature. In other words, the distinction between internal and external is different from the distinction between innate or not innate. In saying so, Gaozi clearly has a target in mind: he is trying to explain that it is inappropriate to understand "internal" and "external" as meaning "internal or external to human nature." That is, even though it is reasonable to take the self as the dividing line between internal and external, the "self" in this case is not equivalent to "human nature," such that "internal or external to the self" is not the same thing as "internal or external to human nature." And from Mencius' words we can see that his doctrine of *ren* as internal and *yi* as external assumes that the distinction between what is internal or external to the self is equivalent to the distinction between what is internal or external to human nature.

To defend his position on the externality of *yi* against Mencius' counter-argument, Gaozi uses what looks like an extremely simple analogy: "They are elder, and we venerate them. It is not that they are elder because of us. Similarly, that is white, and we treat it as white, according to its being white externally to us."[6] The thread of Gaozi's argument is easy to understand. If *yi* is venerating elders, what makes them elder is not that they are "elder because of us"; rather it is because "they are elders." Therefore, an elder's elderliness is an objective fact, just like the whiteness of something white: neither derives its definition from me, nor is it "internal" to me. My treating them as white or elder is just a recognition of an objective fact: I treat something as white because it is white; I treat someone as elder because he is elder. In other words, our "treating it as white" or "elder" is only because of "its being white" or "elder externally to us."

To this point Mencius issues the following reply:

> They are different [*yi yu*, (异於)]! The whiteness of a white horse is no different from the whiteness of a white-haired person. But, surely, we do not regard the elderliness of an old horse as being no different from the elderliness of an old person? Furthermore, do you say that the one who is elder is *yi*, or that the one who treats another as elder is *yi*?[7]

The first thing to notice about this passage is that there is a different opinion over how to punctuate the word *yi yu* (异於) at the beginning. Mou Zongsan analyzes the different views and concludes that the first two characters can be omitted without affecting the meaning of the sentence.[8] However, there is another possibility, namely that this passage does not suffer from interpolation or omission. Since the character *yu* (於) can mark the end of a sentence, we can punctuate the text immediately after "异於."[9] That yields the reading I have given above, which has Mencius saying roughly,

> There is a difference! The whiteness of a white horse is the same as the whiteness of a white-haired person, but don't you understand that the elderliness of an old horse is different from the elderliness of an old person? And are you saying that it is the old person who is *yi* or the person who treats that person as elder?

What still has to be explained is how, from Mencius' perspective, his response to Gaozi is supposed to be a successful one. Mencius replies to Gaozi with two rhetorical questions:

(1) The whiteness of a white horse is no different from the whiteness of a white-haired person. But surely we do not regard the elderliness of an old horse as being no different from the elderliness of an old person?

(2) Furthermore, do you say that the one who is elder is *yi*, or that the one who venerates the elder is *yi*?

Let us begin with question (1). In a debate, a rhetorical question is different from a normal interrogative sentence. Unless it is asked ironically, the rhetorical question clearly indicates the position affirmed by the speaker. In question (1) that position is: the whiteness of a white horse is the same as the whiteness of a white-haired person, but the elderliness of an old horse is not the same as the elderliness of an old person. That is, Mencius thinks that Gaozi's example is wrong. Gaozi has drawn an analogy between "elderliness" and "whiteness" and used the "externality of whiteness" to establish the "externality of elderliness" and thus the externality of *yi*. Therefore, he says, "They are elder, and we treat them as elders. It is not that they are elder because of us. Similarly, that is white, and we treat it as white, according to its being white externally to us." To this, Mencius clearly points out that we cannot understand "elderliness" the same way we do "whiteness." This is the key point to his refutation of Gaozi. What then is different about the concepts of "whiteness" and "elderliness"? What makes the whiteness of a white horse the same as the whiteness of a white-haired person is that "whiteness" is a universal concept. That is, "whiteness" is delimited by the realm of things. "What is called white" is abstracted from "white horses," "white-haired persons" and other such particulars. But "elderliness" is different. It is a formalized concept and, unlike "whiteness," is not delimited by a realm of things but rather is a kind of pure relational demonstrative word. Undoubtedly, we cannot abstract a common "elderliness" from the oldness of a horse and the oldness of a person. Or to put it a different way, as a denotative phenomenon, "elderliness" belongs to the activity of intentionality itself; it does not come from the object of intention itself. It is the intention of the person who venerates an elder that constructs the elder's elderliness. By comparison, "whiteness" as denotative phenomenon does not come from the activity of intentionality itself but rather is related to the object of intention. And it should be mentioned that in the part of his debate with Gaozi about "life as what is meant by nature," Mencius also successfully refutes Gaozi by questioning his misunderstanding of "nature" as a universal concept like "whiteness" rather than a formal concept. Thus, we should say that this is a consistent problem in Gaozi's conceptual interpretation.

Connected with this debate's examples, we can say that, just as the whiteness of white jade, white snow or white feathers is the same but the nature of human beings is not the same as that of dogs or cattle, likewise the whiteness of a white horse and a white-haired person is the same but the elderliness of an old horse and an old person are not the same. If "whiteness" as a universal concept corresponds to some objective fact that does not depend on relationships, then "elderliness" as a formal concept must be involved in the relationship between the elder and the person who venerates him. Or we could say that the relationship between the two people constructs the elderliness of the elder, whereas whiteness is not constructed by the relationship between a white thing and the person who treats it as white. Specifically, the elderliness of a horse certainly exists in relation to a young horse, and its elderliness comes from the contrast with the young horse. The elderliness of an elder human being is certainly also relative, and so it might appear that "elderliness" and "whiteness" both denote an objective fact, but, in fact, affirming the fact of "elderliness" requires going back to the relationship between the elder and the person who treats him as elder. For example, for me my parents are elder, but not for my grandparents. Of course, this relativity does not mean that elderliness is not objective. The elder's elderliness is founded not only upon the recognition of the person who treats him as elder but also on a common field in vision in actual ethical life. In other words, the elder's elderliness is founded upon the objective relationship between him and the one who venerates him.

At this point, Mencius has successfully refuted Gaozi's argument that "they are elder, and we venerate them, just as we treat white things as white." Mencius has shown that there is an error in Gaozi's understanding of "elderliness" (corresponding here to *yi*) in that, unlike "whiteness," "elderliness" is not wholly external and objective but is instead tied up in the relationship between the elder and the person who treats him as elder. Mencius' question (2) is clearly a follow-up to that. Since "venerating elders is what is called *yi*," and since elders are only elders in relation to the people who treat them as such, a person who practices *yi* (i.e., the veneration of elders) can only be such in relation to elders. Not only does recognizing elderliness require the involvement of the person who treats him as elder, but also acts of *yi* issue forth from that person, which implies that this person herself has the ability to "venerate elders" and thus that acts of *yi* are internal to her. Or, as Zhao Qi writes in the *Explanatory Notes on the Mencius*, "Elderliness resides in them; treating them as elders resides in us. Thus, *yi* comes from us who treat them as elders, not from the elders." Gaozi had hoped to show that *yi* is external "according to elderliness being external to us," but through his successful refutation of Gaozi's argument, Mencius has shown the internality of *yi*. Putting it differently, Mencius sees *yi*, like *ren*, as rooted in people's original nature.

Such was the two philosophers' first clash over this problem. After being refuted by Mencius, Gaozi attempts a new explanation of the internality of *yi*:

> My younger brother I love; the younger brother of a person from Qin I do not love. I take the explanation for this to lie in me. Hence, I say that it is internal. I venerate an elder person from Chu, but I also venerate my own elder. I take the explanation for this to lie in the elder person. Hence, I say that it is external.

The first thing to notice is that Gaozi's new explanation shares a certain contextual connection with his first disagreement with Mencius. Gaozi originally wanted to establish the externality of *yi* "according to elderliness being external to us," but Mencius' objection to this pointed out that understanding "elderliness" requires that we look to the relationship between elders and the people who venerate them, where elderliness is internally constructed by the latter's realization of the intentionality of their relationship to the elders. Gaozi's new explanation pays particular attention to the relationship between those two parties: I love my younger brother, not the brother of someone from Qin, but I venerate my own elder and also an elder from Chu. From this we can see that Gaozi not only understood Mencius' earlier refutation, but actually acknowledged its cogency, since his new explanation takes the point of Mencius' criticism as its point of departure.

We can follow Gaozi's new line of reasoning by expounding his implicit assertion, as follows:

[Yes, very well, but even if I admit that what you are saying is correct, to understand "elderliness" requires that we look to the relationship between elders and the people who venerate them, there is still good reason for saying that *ren* is internal and yi is external.] I love my own brother, but not the brother of a person from Qin. This is a case of my being concerned with my own [happiness]. But I venerate an elder from Chu as well as my own elder, and that is a case of my being concerned with the elder's [happiness]. Hence, I say that *yi* is external.

After putting aside the examples of "elderliness" and "whiteness," Gaozi challenges Mencius a second time. The speech that follows is often thought trifling, but the actual point of his argument is easily overlooked. Superficially it would seem that the disagreement between them is that Gaozi claims that *ren* is internal but *yi* external, while Mencius says that both are internal. Although that is certainly true, it does not get to the substance and crux of the two philosophers' disagreement. Gaozi's doubts concern first of all Mencius' concept of internal and external; that is, the fundamental division between the two is their different understandings of "internal" and "external." When Gaozi says, "I take this as having to do with my own happiness" as a gloss for "internal," and "having to do with the elder's happiness" for "external," what he actually means is that *ren* being "internal" and *yi* "external" does not mean "internal or external to human beings' nature." Instead, what he has in mind is two different kinds of ethical relationships and two corresponding kinds of virtue. *Ren* is concerned with "my [happiness]" and corresponds to ethical relationships such as those between brothers. *Yi* is concerned with "other people's [happiness]" and corresponds to ethical relationships such as that between young and old. This constitutes his interpretation of *ren* as internal and *yi* as external.

From what Gaozi says we can draw the main line of his critique of Mencius: the first mistake in Mencius' position on the internality of both *ren* and *yi*, is that he misunderstands "internality" as "internal to our nature." That is to say, his theory that "*ren* and *yi* are internal" relies on a mistaken view of internal and external. "Internal to me" and "external to me" do not mean "internal or external to my nature": instead, *ren* and *yi* correspond to different sorts of ethical relationships, the concern of one of which is within and the other without. In summary, Gaozi thinks that Mencius has conflated the question of internality or externality with the question of human nature, something which is mistaken and, therefore, cannot be used to establish the internality of *ren* and *yi* to our nature.

Mencius does not answer this new argument directly but states his position by means of an analogy: "Savoring the roast of a person from Qin is no different from savoring my own roast. So, it is also thus with objects. Is savoring a roast, then, also external?" Mencius' answer is not so easy to understand, even at the level of literal meaning. Let us analyze it bit by bit. To begin with, what does he mean by saying, "Savoring the roast of a person from Qin is no different from savoring my own roast?" Unfolding Mencius' implicit argument here will help clarify his ideas. Mencius' point here is nothing other than this: even though "the roast of a person from Qin" and "my own roast" have different owners, the person from Qin and I are both people, and our roasts are both roasts. What this means is that the two roasts are no different from each other in respect of their being savored by people, which is to say, in respect of their flavor. To put it differently, "savoring his roast" and "savoring my own roast" are both cases of savoring, and the fundamental reason is that mouths have the same tastes. This is what Mencius means by saying, "Savoring the roast of a person from Qin is no different from savoring my own roast." And as for the next sentence, "So, it is also thus with objects," the "thus" is clearly denoting the roasts, and "objects" is inferred from "roasts." So, what was said earlier about roasts can be applied to any "objects" in the usual sense. Mencius is thereby universalizing from roasts to objects in general: any type of object, insofar as it can become an object of human desire, depends mainly on humans' shared ability to desire.

Lastly, and most importantly, we have to clarify the meaning of "Is savoring a roast, then, also external?" As we have already stated, desire is always grounded to an internal faculty, and it is the use of this shared human ability to desire (that is, the common desiring activity) that makes an "entity" a desired "object." Thus, despite a desire's object being external and this relationship involving all different kinds of entities, we cannot say that desire itself is external, so, in a word, the "savor" of "savoring a roast" can be explained only from the perspective of the internal ability to desire.

The example of savoring a roast is, as we know, an analogy Mencius used to answer Gaozi, and so what we need to grasp ultimately is the force of that analogy. Clearly, "the roast of a person from Qin" and "my own roast" correspond to "an elder from Chu" and "my own elders" and "savoring" corresponds to "venerating elder." From the analysis above, we can sum up the point of Mencius' counter-argument as follows: "venerating an elder from Chu" and "venerating my own elder" are no different in respect of venerating someone, even though the object of the veneration is different. In the same way, "savoring the roast of a person from Qin" and "savoring my own roast" are no different in respect of savoring something, even though the object is different. Therefore, we cannot say that "elderliness" is external, since the ability to venerate is internal to the person who does so. Likewise, we cannot say that "savoring" is external, since the ability to savor is internal to the savorer. According to Mencius' view, no matter whether I am venerating an elder from Chu or my own elder, the crucial point lies in the venerator's activity of veneration, and that activity is rooted in the venerator's internal ability to venerate. If what is being manifested in the action of veneration is *yi*, then we cannot say that *yi* is external, for it is precisely the operation of the venerator's internal ability to desire that results in a righteous (*yi*) behavior. Righteous behavior is rooted in the internal, inherent ability to desire, which is to say, in human nature. As we can see, Mencius' counter-argument does not directly address the case of "loving one's brother rather than the brother of someone from Qin" but rather that of "venerating an elder from Chu as well as my own elder." Straightforwardly speaking, even though "love" and "veneration" have their differences, both are rooted in people's internal, inherent ability to desire, or in human nature. In this regard, we cannot then say that *ren* is internal and *yi* external; rather, both are internal. "Venerating an elder from Chu and one's own elder" are not actually things that "have to do with the elder's happiness" but rather "have to do with my happiness," as in the case of "loving one's brother," where the "happiness" has its source in human nature. "Love" and "veneration" or "respect" rooted in human nature (or, in other words, *ren* and *yi*) are both things that "make our minds happy." With this, Mencius has returned to his consistent view that *ren* and *yi* are "inherent in me."

It needs to be pointed out that Mencius' emphasis on the internality of *ren* and *yi* does not mean that he denies the fact that they always involve an external object. In fact, what creates acts of *ren* and *yi* is precisely their issuing forth outwardly from people's inward nature. In his commentary to the passage of dialogue between Gaozi and Mencius about "the desires for food and sex as our nature," Sun Shi writes: "This section asserts that, although actions accord with what is external, the performing conduct originates from the center, and this explains that *ren* and *yi* [come from] within. Thus, Gaozi's misunderstanding is evident."[10] That is to say, the abilities to love and respect are internal to me, though the objects of that love and respect are of course external. The abilities are both internal, though the things—the objects that are loved and respected—are both external. Gaozi's mistake is to pair "love" with "object of respect" and then claim on that basis that "*ren* is internal and *yi* external." Clearly, we could even arrive at the mistaken conclusion that *ren* is *external* and *yi* internal if we just inverted things and paired "object of love" with "respect." And in fact, we can see much this kind of point in the *Mozi*'s criticism of the doctrine that *ren* is internal and *yi* external:

> *Ren* equates with love; and *yi* equates with benefit. Love and benefit relate to "this" [the self]. What is loved and what is benefited relate to "that" [the other]. Love and benefit are neither internal nor external; what is loved and what is benefited are neither external nor internal. To say that *ren* is internal and *yi* is external and to conflate love with what is benefited are examples of "wild raising."[11]

Though Mozi's interpretation of *yi* as "benefit" sets him apart from the standpoint of Confucianism, with its emphatic distinction between those two concepts, his criticism here of the doctrine that *ren* is internal and *yi* external reveals a pertinent point. Indeed, it affords us a glimpse of an extremely serious consequence of that doctrine, namely that it makes *ren* and *yi* into two separate things, each with a separate basis.[12]

We still have one issue to discuss concerning the interpretation of this debate. Gaozi and Mencius are discussing the question about the internality and externality of *ren* and *yi* in connection with their differing views of human nature, but how is Mencius attempting to use the example of "savoring a roast" to answer Gaozi's argument? As we have already noted, Gaozi's position is that Mencius has conflated the question of human nature with the question of internality and externality, resulting in his belief that *ren* and *yi* are human nature. And we also know that Gaozi's core view on human nature is that "the desires for food and sex are our nature." From this we can see that, by adducing an example having to do with the desire for food, Mencius is directly answering Gaozi's remarks on human nature. The first thing to point out is that it would be overly general to say simply that Mencius disagrees with Gaozi that "the desires for food and sex are our nature." To the contrary, in fact, Mencius to a certain extent does not deny Gaozi's point, as he says:

> The mouth in relation to flavors, the eyes in relation to sights, the ears in relation to notes, the nose in relation to odors, the four limbs in relation to comfort—these are matters of human nature, but they are also fated. Nonetheless a gentleman does not refer to them as "human nature."[13]

This is to say, the desires for food and sex, and also *ren* and *yi*, are all decreed by Heaven: hence, they can all be classified as belonging to human nature (since "what is decreed by Heaven is called our nature"), but since "the gentleman carries on his conduct according to Heaven (*li ming*, 立命) by nurturing and preserving his nature (*cun xing*, 存性)," he must differentiates between the two, reckoning *ren* and *yi* as human nature and the desire for food and sex as decreed by Heaven. This implies that Mencius to some extent accepts Gaozi's view of the desire for food and sex as human nature. Thus, Mencius' choice of "savoring a roast" as his example subtly contains a deeper level of criticism of Gaozi, i.e., for even if I admit that the desires for food and sex belong to human nature, one cannot say that these "desires" are external, despite the terrific variety of wonderful flavors and sights that are the objects of those desires. Moreover, fundamentally it is humanity's common tastes which cause certain things to appeal to us. If flavor and appearance are among a thing's qualities, then, on the one hand, these qualities rely on people's sensory abilities, and on the other, the attractiveness of the flavor or appearance cannot be called qualities of the thing since they come from humanity's common tastes.

There is little new material in Gongduzi's debate with Gaozi's disciple Meng Jizi, but there are some significant points that make it worth a simple summary. First, it is in this part of the narrative that we get a very explicit explanation of the "internality of *yi*"—"I act out of my respect, and hence I say that it is internal"—which is entirely consonant with our earlier clarification of the meaning of the internality of *yi*. Even though the object of respect is external, the ability to respect is internal, and hence *yi* is said to be internal because of people's inner ability that makes acts of *yi* possible. Next, Meng Jizi adduces the case of "respecting one's eldest brother but pouring wine for a fellow villager first" from ethical life to begin a line of argument for the externality of *yi*, differentiating "respect for fellow villager" from "respecting one's eldest brother" as "the one whom you venerate" and "the one whom you respect." Here "respecting a fellow villager" is supposed to be a case of *yi* and "respecting one's eldest brother" a case of *ren*, something essentially identical to Gaozi's examples of "loving my brother rather than the brother of someone from Qin" for *ren* and "venerating an elder from Chu as well as my own elder" for *yi*, even though Meng Jizi is using the verb "respect" in both cases. And when he says, "The one you venerate is there" and "the one you respect is here," the "there" and "here" correspond to external and internal: the distinction he is making is between the "internality of *ren*" and the "externality of *yi*." And this argument, of course, is the reason that "Gongduzi was not able to answer." So, the challenge for Mencius now is how to explain why one respects one's eldest brother but serves a fellow villager first in a way that is at least compatible with the internality of both *ren* and *yi*. Mencius' response is extremely clear. He notes that ordinarily one shows respect to one's uncle, not one's younger brother, except when the younger brother is playing the role of the deceased in a sacrifice, as a way of explaining the reason that one respects one's eldest brother but, when drinking wine, serves a fellow villager first: "It has to do with the roles people occupy. Ordinary respect is directed toward my brother, but temporary respect is directed toward the fellow villager." The implicit significance is that the difference between the two is not that one is the eldest brother and the other a fellow villager but instead the difference is in the roles they occupy in actual ethical life, or the difference between "ordinarily" and "temporarily." This also makes clear that different ethical settings imply different behavioral orientations and these differences are fittingly depicted in different circumstances. Clearly this explanation does not have a direct connection to the position that *ren* is internal and *yi* external; it just counters a case put forward in favor of the opposing position.[14] Therefore, after Meng Jizi heard this from Gongduzi, he confronted him, saying that, "Regardless of whether it is your uncle or your younger brother, it is the same manifestation of respect. So, it really is external. It does not come from how you feel internally."

On a closer examination, what Meng Jizi means is that one respects an uncle because he is one's uncle, whereas one respects one's younger brother because he is playing the role of the deceased. Or, more precisely, there would be no reason to respect the younger brother if he were not playing the deceased. Does this not mean that respect is external? Gongduzi's response to this is basically correct: drinks are external, of course, no matter whether hot broth or water, but the ability to drink is internal. In the same way, the object of respect is of course external, no matter whether it is one's uncle or younger brother, but the ability to respect is internal.

To summarize what has been said above, the point of Mencius' doctrine that *ren* and *yi* are both internal is to emphasize that they are the same inasmuch as they both emerge from human nature. But this does not mean there is no difference between *ren* and *yi*, only that the difference is not that one is internal and the other one external. Rather, it emerges from different ethical settings. The different virtues have a common source in human nature: this means that they can avoid the "two sources" problem, and also lays a possible foundation for the unity of those virtues. Therefore, a perfect portrayal of the situation would be the concept of an ethical "heart-mind" that governs all the virtues. Different ethical settings call for different goods, which call for different virtues. This requires that the heart-mind employ "reflection" (which is "the function of the heart-mind," as Mencius says in 6A.15) to arrive at a careful synthesis appropriate to an actual, temporalized situation. (And, of course, there is no need to say that the "heart-mind" in this case is a practical, ethical mind.) Aside from his reasonable recognition of the diversity of good, Mencius argues for the commonality of human responses to good, or what he calls "what [heart-]minds prefer in common."[15] And the commonality in Mencius' and Gaozi's thinking is a theme that is fairly important but consistently overlooked.

It has never been noticed before that Mencius explains his view that "the sages and we are of the same kind" in terms of commonality of tastes. In order to present this view in context, a passage from the *Mencius* is in order:

> Mencius said, "In years of plenty, most young men are gentle; in years of poverty, most young men are violent. It is not that the potential that Heaven confers on them varies like this. They are like this because of what sinks and drowns their hearts. Consider barley. Sow the seeds and cover them. The soil is the same and the time of planting is also the same. They grow rapidly, and by the time of the summer solstice they have all ripened. Although there are some differences, these are due to the richness of the soil and to unevenness in the rain and in human effort. Hence, in general, things of the same kind are similar. Why would one have any doubt about this when it comes to humans alone? We and the sage are of the same kind. Hence, Longzi said, 'When one makes a sandal for a foot one has not seen, we know that one will not make a basket.' The similarity of all the shoes in the world is due to the fact that the feet of the world are the same.

> "Mouths have the same taste in flavors. Master Chef Yi Ya was the first to discover what our mouths prefer. If it were the case that the natures of mouths varied among people—just as dogs and horses are different species from us—then how could it be that throughout the world all tastes

follow Yi Ya when it comes to flavor? When it comes to flavor, the reason the whole world looks to Yi Ya is that tastes throughout the world are similar.

"Ears are like this too. When it comes to sounds, the whole world looks to Music Master Shi Kuang. This is because ears throughout the world are similar. Eyes are like this too. No one in the world does not appreciate the handsomeness of a man like Zidu. Anyone who does not appreciate the handsomeness of Zidu does not have eyes. Hence, I say that mouths have the same tastes in flavors, ears have the same tastes in sounds, eyes have the same tastes in attractiveness. When it comes to [heart-]minds, are they alone without any tastes in common?

"What is it that [heart-]minds prefer in common? I say that it is order and righteousness. The sages first discovered what our minds prefer in common. Hence, order and righteousness delight our [heart-]minds like meat delights our mouths."[16]

It seems that we could easily object that in actuality people's tastes are not really identical. However, Mencius' point is deeply significant. Although scholars often quote such famous lines as "the sages and we are of the same kind" and "order and righteousness delight our [heart-]minds like meat delights our mouths," the true significance of something like "the common-ality between the sages and ourselves" is extremely easy to overlook. In other words, there are many circumstances under which simply mentioning this view without going into a detailed explanation can amount to creating a false impression by quoting without any regard to the context.

Although we may state, in a very general way, that Mencius' view that "the sages and we are of the same kind" is built upon a concept of a universal human nature, as we can see from the passage above, what he really means is this: not only do people's senses of taste, sound and sight "have something they prefer in common" (mouths, ears and eyes have the same tastes in flavors, sounds and sights), but in addition, people's mental consciousness also "has something they prefer in common": "What is it that [heart-]minds prefer in common? I say that it is order and righteousness." (Or we might say, "[Heart-]minds have the same tastes in goodness.") It seems, then, that "mental con-sciousness" is a unique type of awareness that is intimately related to thought and knowledge ("the function of heart-mind is to reflect"), and hence we can differentiate mental consciousness from ordinary sensory awareness. The first thing to clarify is that it is misleading to say in general terms that Mencius is claiming that there is a commonality between sensing and mental conscious-ness. His main point here is not to show that sense and mental conscious-ness prove to be the same, like showing that people all experience vinegar as sour-tasting. In fact, a true understanding of Mencius' point here has to make use of the concept of "taste." That is, whether we are talking mouths and flavors, ears and sounds, eyes and sights or heart-minds and goodness, we are speaking of the commonality of taste. And commonality of taste can only come from *community* of taste. Therefore, it might be more appropriate to describe Mencius' position this way: our perception of things that delight our mouths, ears, eyes and even heart-minds are communal. No discussion of a doctrine of the community of taste can fail to mention the concept of the *sensus communis*. In fact, we might even say that what we see in the passages above is Mencius' theory of *sensus communis*.

Tastes can be divided into the good and the bad. Affirming a community of taste means that people's sensory and mental awareness of the goodness or badness of taste is communal. Everyone can experience the sourness in a given bottle of vinegar, but this has nothing to do with the problem of taste. It implies a judgment of taste and for taste to constitute a judgment requires some *sensus communis* as its prerequisite. In other words, the foundation for communality of perceptions of the goodness or badness of tastes is a *sensus communis*. But does that really exist? Is humankind really unanimous in its tastes? We often see what seems to be the very opposite. Whether within a particular community or across different communities, there exists a gigantic gulf in tastes, not only with respect to the senses of taste, hearing and sight but also in our perceptions of what is good. The key to correctly understanding the significance of *sensus communis* is to not simply to try to explain community of tastes by resorting to the universality of experience. The possibility of judgments of taste is not built upon actual common experience but on some kind of possibility of imperative or normative force. That is to say, *sensus communis* does not mean that every person has the same actual tastes. In Kant's words, a judgment of taste "contains an ought": "it does not say that everyone *will* agree with my judgment but that he *ought* to."[17] It must be emphasized that, just as we pointed out above, commonality of tastes can only come from community of tastes. This "community" really refers to "communicability." That is, the commonality of tastes that we refer to as *sensus communis* actually comes from the communicability of tastes which is the principal factor in allowing tastes to constitute judgments.[18]

As for where the imperative or normative force to judgments of taste comes from (which is to say, the source of the *sensus communis* itself), there are two kinds of explanation: one relies on the communality of people's perceptual tendencies, while the other relies on the uniformity of the community's influence on people's perceptual tendencies. The first is fundamentally an anthropological explanation. Just as in Mencius, the communality of perceptual tendencies can be explained using a concept of universal human nature—that is, as group traits of humankind. Of course, it would be reasonable to take this sort of view—which we might call a type of "philosophical anthropology"—and add on a religious or theological condition. For example, if we brought in the doctrine of "what is decreed by Heaven is our nature," then we could reasonably say that the *sensus communis* fundamentally comes from Heaven's decree. Or to give another example, the Stoics' conception of the *sensus communis* had a sense of "natural right," and eighteenth-century German Lutheran theologian F.C. Oetinger called the *sensus communis* a "gift from God."[19] Kant's approach to *sensus communis* is also anthropological in a sense, since he believes it is "the effect arising from the free play of our cognitive powers" and says even more explicitly that it is "the (mutual) quickening of the two mental powers" of humanity's imagination and understanding.[20] The problem with this approach is that, even if there is nothing deficient in calling the communality of perceptual tendencies the source of the *sensus communis*, it still ignores certain dimensions. A classic illustration of this is Kant's understanding of the *sensus communis*, which Gadamer criticizes for its tendency to abstraction and thorough subjectivization, since Kant denies that judgments of taste have any significance as knowledge. This means that *sensus communis* and judgments of taste that are grounded on it lack objective relations and "[impart] no knowledge of an object."[21] They are confined to freely coordinating the activities of the emotional level of the subject's epistemic capacity.

To explain the unanimity of judgments of better taste, many thinkers have tended to link the concept of *sensus communis* with that of community. Vico, for example, explained nations in terms of *sensus communis*, and Hannah Arendt used it to help explain the public nature of political space. And Gadamer emphasized the originally ethical character of *sensus communis*, writing that "the moral and historical existence of humanity, as it takes shape in our words and deeds, is itself decisively determined by the *sensus communis*."[22] It is very noteworthy that Gadamer traces the concept of *sensus communis* back to Aristotle, taking it as a footnote to his belief that "man is by nature a political animal." Specifically, its significance is manifest not only in the importance of Aristotle's *polis* to practical life but even more importantly in his famous distinction between *phronesis* and *sophia*. The key to this view is that it draws the imperative or normative force of the *sensus communis* or judgments of taste together with the practical life of the community. In other words, the existence of social mores is the essential precondition for *sensus communis*, and the status of *phronesis* as a kind of knowledge directly related to the existence of social mores is born precisely out of *sensus communis*. Thus, the existence of social mores, *sensus communis* and *phronesis* constitutes a hermeneutic circle. This means that taking the *phronesis* based on *sensus communis* as a kind of knowledge (that is, as having epistemic significance) is the true source of a certain kind of truth and knowledge. Of course, it must emphatically be pointed out that this kind of *phronesis* differs from *sophia* in that it is temporary and probabilistic. *Phronesis* is not knowledge of an eternal object but probabilistic knowledge that emerges amid the changing circumstances of everyday living, connected to practical particular actions. That is to say, the objects of *phronesis* are pragmatic affairs that are by their nature ever-changing and are intimately related to the existence of social mores. Thus, knowledge of the good can only be transient and probabilistic. This was the principal reason that Aristotle objected to Plato's "idea of the good," since Platonic ideas are precisely supposed to be eternal things. For just this reason, Gadamer points out, in Western history, taste based on *sensus communis* "was originally more a *moral* idea," linked to the idea of the perfect person and to a social function, that "[described] an ideal of genuine humanity," for which reason Gadamer classified Aristotle's ethics as "an ethics of good taste."[23]

There is an obvious tension between these two vastly different-looking kinds of accounts of the source of *sensus communis*. The first kind, which traces it to a group trait, links *sensus communis* to the universality of human nature, no matter whether it explains that as a fact of nature or something ordained by God. In contrast, the second sort of account, which explains *sensus communis* in terms of the community, traces it to the unique nature of that community, particularly when the account acknowledges the fact of cultural pluralism. Gadamer pointed out that "the old Roman concept of *sensus communis*" had an obviously critical flavor and

> when faced with Greek culture, held firmly to the value and significance of their own traditions of civil and social life. A critical note directed against the theoretical speculations of the philosophers can be heard in the Roman concept of the *sensus communis*.[24]

An account based on human traits seems to offer a way that *sensus communis* can transcend community boundaries; a community-based account seems to dispel the mist of abstract universalism and better explain the imperative and normative force of *sensus communis*. Since, as already pointed out, commonality of taste is not an empirical universal but rather comes from the communality or communicability of taste, this tension is not only understandable but can even be something positive. The key here is that we could not take the community as something ready-made. This implies not just that the real lives of communities are ever-shifting but also that communities really are communal bodies. They move towards maturity as they cultivate and mold good taste. *Sensus communis* creates real community, and the community provides the real space for *sensus communis*.

What we see in Mencius is clearly the first approach. From what our senses "have in common" he deduces what "our heart-minds prefer in common." That is, Mencius sees the commonalities in our sensory awareness as the easier ones to explain. The commonalities in our mental awareness are not so apparent and have to be explained by analogy to the senses. From this we can see the true import of Mencius' view that "the sages and we are of the same kind," namely that the sages and we have tastes in common, in sensory awareness and in mental awareness. In other words, human beings' senses and heart-minds have things in common, and if we want to account for why that is, we must do so in terms of a universal human nature. It may seem peculiar to use the idea of "taste" to conceptualize "the order and righteousness that delight our heart-minds," but this is only because in modern times "taste" has receded into nothing more than an aesthetic concept. So even though using the notion of "taste" here can shed some light from a new angle on the true import of Mencius' remarks, in order to avoid unnecessary confusion, we can also express it in a different way. To wit, humankind has a communal and indeed a common sense of the good. That is, humanity shares a communal and common ethical signification. This view is unsurpassably important for understanding Confucian ethical thought. For someone like Mou Zongsan who looks at Confucianism in moralistic terms, the interpretive strategy here is to appropriate the Kantian concepts of moral interest or moral pleasure for use in his own explanation of Mencius' "order and righteousness that delight our heart-minds."[25] It needs to be pointed out here that this understanding still reduces ethics to abstract morality. That is, for Mencius the "order and righteousness" that delight our heart-minds are not abstract moral principles but rather are grounded on principles of human relations that are particular and personal. And, therefore, the "delight" that our heart-minds get from order and righteousness are, unlike Kant's moral interest or moral pleasure, built on true, personal joy in the human relations ordained by Heaven.

Notes

1 *Mencius* 6A.4–5. See Philip J. Ivanhoe and Bryan W. Van Norden (eds.), *Readings in Classical Chinese Philosophy* (Hackett Publishing, 2005, pp. 145–147. Translation adapted from Van Norden's.
2 Translation adapted from Kenneth Holloway, *Guodian: The Newly Discovered Seeds of Chinese Religious and Political Philosophy* (Oxford University Press, 2009), p. 35.
3 This point was raised by Wang Bo, who distinguishes three versions of the doctrine that *ren* is internal and *yi* external and believes that Mencius would only agree with the first, in which internal and external refer to the family. See his "Early Confucianism's Theory on Ren and Yi," *Peking University Journal of Philosophy*, 2005 (11), p. 87, n. 27.
4 *Mencius* 6A.6. See Ivanhoe and Van Norden, *Readings in Classical Chinese Philosophy*, pp. 147–148.
5 *Mencius* 6A.1. See Ivanhoe and Van Norden, *Readings in Classical Chinese Philosophy*, p. 144
6 *Mencius* 6A.4. See Ivanhoe and Van Norden, *Readings in Classical Chinese Philosophy*, pp. 145–146.
7 *Mencius* 6A.4.
8 Mou Zongsan writes:

> Zhu's commentary mentions that Zhang Shi suggested that the characters "异於" at the beginning of this passage might be an interpolation, and also that Li Tong (?) thought there might be an omission here. Zhao Qi's commentary puts punctuation after "异於白" and continues "马之白也无以异於白人之白也." But that results in a not-ordered wording style and incomplete grammar. Furthermore, in "白马之白也无以异於白人之白也," "白" is clearly an adjective. But if we did not follow Zhao's punctuation, the sentence would read "白马之白也无以异於白人之白也," following the "白之" ["treating it as white"] in the preceding sentence, "彼白而我白之." In that way the "白" in "白马" and "白人" becomes a verb, just like the "长" in the "长马" and "长人" in the following sentence. This is the only reading that fits and makes sense of Mencius' objection, but Zhao Qi's punctuation turns the "白" into an adjective, thus objecting the sense of Mencius' question, and so I do not follow his reading. If we must suppose that there are omissions in the text, then we should amend it to read: (长之之长) 异於 (白之之白). This would make

sense but is unnecessary. Thus, for simplicity's sake we can take the first two characters as interpolations and omit them, as the meaning of the sentence is already abundantly clear.

(Mou Zongsan, *Treatise on the Summum Bonum*, pp. 12–13)

9 In fact, the text has already been read this way. See Pei Xuehai, *Gushu xuzi jishi* [*Collective Explanations on Empty Words of Ancient Texts*], Vol. 1. (Zhonghua Book Company, 2004), p. 61.

10 *Notes and Commentaries on Mencius*, Vol. 2 (Zhonghua Book Company, 1980), p. 2764.

11 From *Explanations II*. Translation adapted from Ian Johnston (trans.), *The Mozi: A Complete Translation* (Columbia University Press, 2010), p. 567.

12 When Mencius criticizes the Mohist Yi Zhi's opinion that "love is without differentiations, but it is bestowed beginning with one's parents," he says, "Heaven, in giving birth to things, causes them to have one source, but Yi Zhi gives them two sources." (Ivanhoe and Van Norden, *Readings in Classical Chinese Philosophy*, p. 7). What he means is that, following Yi Zhi's argument, universal love would need to have one source and love for one's parents another; the two would have no common basis. Similarly, the position that "love for one's parents" (corresponding to *ren*) is internal and "respect for elders" (corresponding to *yi*) is external can hardly avoid this absurdity of two sources.

13 *Mencius* 7B.24. See Ivanhoe and Van Norden, *Readings in Classical Chinese Philosophy*, p. 155.

14 It is worth noting that Mencius' explanation could naturally involve further questions about what he means by "ordinarily." Also, the difference between "ordinary respect" and "temporary respect" could be compared to that between the constant and the provisional.

15 "Have in common in mind" (*Mencius* 6A.7). See Ivanhoe and Van Norden, *Readings in Classical Chinese Philosophy*, p. 149.

16 *Mencius* 6A.7. See Ivanhoe and Van Norden, *Readings in Classical Chinese Philosophy*, pp. 148–149.

17 Immanuel Kant, *Critique of Judgement*, trans. by Werner Pluhar (Hackett Publishing, 1987), p. 239.

18 I believe this is the reason that scholars of earlier generations translated *sensus communis* as共通感rather than共同感, as the former translation really conveys the essence of the concept.

19 See Hans-Georg Gadamer, *Truth and Method*, trans. by Joel Weinsheimer and Donald G. Marshall, 2nd rev. ed. (Continuum, 2004), p. 27.

20 Kant, *Critique of Judgement*, p. 238.

21 Gadamer, *Truth and Method*, p. 37.

22 Gadamer, *Truth and Method*, p. 20.

23 Gadamer, *Truth and Method*, pp. 31, 35.

24 Gadamer, *Truth and Method*, p. 20.

25 Kant distinguishes "pathological interest" from "moral interest," as well as "pathological pleasure" from "moral pleasure."

7 "The internality of benevolence and righteousness" and autonomous morality

Mou Zongsan believes that Mencius' doctrine of "benevolence and righteousness are found within" best reflects the Confucian advocation of autonomous morality. He not only affirms autonomous morality but also approves autonomous morality at the high level of Confucian orthodoxy, regarding it as essential for the establishment of Confucian orthodoxy:

> "Benevolence and righteousness are found within" is not easy to comprehend. As in the Western theories of morality, heteronomy dominated before Kant, but autonomy became predominant since him. In China, ever since Mencius took the initiative to advocate "benevolence and righteousness are found within" to denounce Gaozi's position, only Lu Jiuyuan and Wang Yangming inherited what he advocated without diverging from his meaning, thus effectively understanding the fundamental point of his theory. Other thinkers, like Cheng Yi and Zhu Xi, have gone astray. Though they did not deviate from his thought, they failed to comprehend it as Lu Jiuyuan and Wang Yangming did. However, if one does not grasp the meaning of "benevolence and righteousness are found within," he or she will not set the foundation for the theory of the goodness of human nature.[1]

Autonomous morality as the fundamental feature of Confucianism has brought about some external criticism, but it is widely recognized by Confucian scholars, it exerted a profound influence, and it is known as "the most groundbreaking interpretation of Confucianism in contemporary Chinese thought."[2]

To elucidate the internality of benevolence and righteousness based on the concept of moral autonomy does not seem to need evidence. Because, when the benevolence and righteousness correspond to the *nomos* (rule, norm) which is the principle of morality, and the internality corresponds to the *auto*, namely, freedom and autonomy, the above interpretation seems to be well-grounded. Thus, the internality of benevolence and righteousness is interpreted as how human beings actively and freely regulate themselves with morality. Based on this insight, Mou Zongsan introduced the distinctions between "fact" and "value," and between knowledge and morality, to explain the two stages of Mencius and Gaozi's debate on internal benevolence and external righteousness.

On the first stage of the debate between Mencius and Gaozi, Mou Zongsan's crucial point is that the whiteness of a white horse and a white man is fact: that is, it is related to knowledge of the horse and the man, while the elderliness of an old horse and an old man is value: that is, it is related to the moral attitude to the horse and the man. Mou Zongsan states that:

> obviously, for the old horse, although I treat it as an old horse and show mercy to it, I have no respect for it, while for the old man, I regard him as elderly with respect. They are not the same. This is obviously different when we look at the matter of whiteness of the white horse and the white man. White is a matter of fact, while showing respect for the elderly is a moral issue.[3]

It seems that the explanation is reasonable, but actually it is entirely wrong. First of all, Mou Zongsan does not understand the meaning of Mencius' refutation. As mentioned before, what Mencius stresses here is that the concepts of "white" and "old" (another core argument is "nature") do not belong to the same conceptual category. We can say that "the whiteness of a white horse has no difference with the whiteness of the white man," but we cannot say that "the elderliness of an old horse is the same with the elderliness of an old man." Similarly, we cannot say "the nature of a dog is like that of an ox, and the nature of an ox is like the nature of a man." The reason is that the whiteness of a white horse and a white man is a general concept, while the elderliness of an old horse and old man is a formal concept; the former is clearly defined by the specific content, while the latter denotes an interconnection. The difference between "mercy" and "respect" pointed out by Mou Zongsan to illustrate the difference between the "old horse" and the "old man" is an entirely subjective interpretation. The difference related to the elderliness of an old horse and that of an old man does not lie in different moral attitudes towards old people and an old horse inherent to a moral subject. Instead, in order to understand the term "old" in the two, we need to investigate the relation between old and young related to the old horse as old horse and the old man as an old man. The reason why the elderliness is different in relation to an old horse and an old man, is that the young and old relations of the two are different. Secondly, it is nonsense to argue that the elderliness of an old horse and an old man has nothing to do with knowledge. The formal concept itself also constitutes a formal sign of knowledge or truth. When we say, "this horse is an old horse" or "this man is an old man," is not that a kind of assertion related to the acknowledgment of the horse or the man? Is not this a true or false judgment about the horse or the man? Besides, the distinction between "fact" and "value" is a historical reflection inherent to the Western ethical world recently risen in the West, and its forced application to Chinese thinkers of the pre-Qin period is rather inappropriate. The key here is not that there may be a misinterpretation due to the chronological difference, nor is it a methodological issue related to "interpreting China according to the Western paradigm," but lies in what is implicit in the distinction between fact and value. The distinction between fact and value is not just a matter of logic, as Hume claimed. In fact, the distinction between fact and value means differentiation within the living world. Whether for a person, or for a nation, the dichotomy of "yes" and "should" means that this person or the nation can no longer unify the existence and the essence of himself or itself. The contradiction between existence and essence no longer works as a positive force, but only reflects a passive "present-at-hand" (*Vorhandenheit*), at the ultimate expense of the loss in essence.

On the first round of the debate between Mencius and Gaozi, Mou Zongsan does not think Mencius' refutation is successful. For "savoring the roast meat" cited by Mencius, Mou Zongsan puts forward the objection that "this example by Mencius is a matter of common sense. In fact, 'savoring the roast meat' is a matter of taste, and people do not have the same taste, so the same enjoyment is not necessary."[4] This is a rather rash comment, indicating that Mou Zongsan does not understand the true connotation of the "the Sage and we are the same in kind," thus missing Mencius' idea of universality. If we are unable to truly understand the universality or interconnection of beauty and kindness advocated by Mencius, it will be impossible to truly understand the "principle and righteousness" inherent to "the principles of our nature and the determination of righteousness are agreeable to my mind" (*yi li zhi yue wo xin*, 理义之悦我心). Concerning Gaozi's standpoint, Mou Zongsan summarizes and comments that:

> his point is that righteousness depends on objective facts, so it is external. Whatever the object is, I should say what it is. This righteousness of "ought to be" derives from the objective fact, which can be determined by cognitive knowledge, and also can assume that "righteousness means appropriateness." For example, fur is appropriate during winter, and hemp clothing is appropriate during summer, all of which has no moral significance. Benevolence should be about morality, but that factual attitude repeatedly cited by Gaozi gradually misses the moral significance of "righteousness."[5]

According to Mou Zongsan, the focus of Mencius and Gaozi's argument here is the difference between knowledge and morality, or the difference between fact and value. The above analysis shows that Mencius is not refusing the aspect related to the objective fact of achievement and virtuous conduct of benevolence. Whether it is the benevolence reflected in "loving relatives," or the righteousness reflected in "respecting the elder," this is precisely based on certain objective facts ("relatives" or "elder people"). We honor our parents first because they *are* our parents, and we *are* their sons. Likewise, our concern about our friend, first of all, is because he or she is our friend. Ignoring the objective fact inherent to "are" or "*is*" and advocating a moral concern without implying a factual-existential basis for that do not conform to the spirit of Mencius or even Confucianism. What Mencius hopes to make clear is that, as a moral virtue, benevolence has its roots in human nature, and its inherent causes shall not be denied just because achievement and virtuous conduct are acknowledged outward. But Mencius does not develop his theory to the other extreme, that is, stating that the moral conduct of benevolence completely ignores objective existence. If shared human nature is based on the commonality inherent to these two virtues, "benevolence" and "righteousness," then the difference between "benevolence" and "righteousness" has to be ascribed to the difference between their corresponding objective entities. The fully internalized explanation of Mencius' thought proposed by Mou Zongsan is improper. It can reasonably be assumed that the idea of "righteousness means appropriateness" would be accepted by Mencius. His annotation on "righteousness means appropriateness" cannot simply be understood as the "ought to be" like "fur is appropriate during winter, and hemp clothing is appropriate during summer." "Ought to be" is none other than a mode of representation for "to be." Only by making a detailed inquiry on the self-authentic being and the self-constitutive goods can one gain more genuine knowledge of the "ought to be" in ethical life.

In relation to the debate between Meng Ji and Gongduzi, Mou Zongsan once again made an explanation based on the distinction between knowledge and morality, fact and value. Even though, on the one hand, the consistency of these arguments' interpretation reveals the continuity of Mou Zongsan's line of thought, on the other hand, it is still a misunderstanding. Mou Zongsan points out the reason why Meng Ji sticks to the standpoint of "righteousness is external," even though this point was refuted by Mencius, by stating that "he regards his uncle as an entity in ethical relations." It should be noted that this generalization is completely correct. However, he then remarks that Meng Ji's problem is that he misunderstands the value of moral human relations as an objective fact:

> However, even though moral human relations originate from the human moral mind, the patriarchal hierarchy is ruled in this way. This is a matter related to the value of humanity. The mind cannot grasp the reason why the value is established, which can never be understood within righteousness.[6]

In this regard, on the one hand, we could reply that "However, even the moral mind must act by following the objective entity of ethical relations; on the other hand, the argument that the moral mind determines patriarchal hierarchy and sage hierarchy is taking the branch for the root. As for the final reply of Gongduzi, Mou Zongsan claimed that it is incongruous. As explained above, Gongduzi's reply intends to explain the difference between "respect" and "the people respected" by stressing the difference between "eating and drinking" and "what we eat and drink", which is basically consistent with the rhetorical question "will you say likewise that our enjoyment of roast is external?" in the debate with Gaozi.

We now analyze why Mou Zongsan introduce the distinction between fact and value, knowledge and moral, in order to explain the debate on internality or externality of benevolence and righteousness between Mencius and Gaozi. Because autonomy is always established in contrast to heteronomy, when Mou Zongsan explains Mencius' point that "righteousness is internal" as moral autonomy, he also interprets "righteousness is external" as moral heteronomy. By introducing the distinction between fact and value, knowledge and morality, Mou Zongsan illustrates the difference between Mencius and Gaozi further, that is, the former stands for an autonomous morality while the latter stands for a heteronomous morality.

In Kant's moral philosophy, the key difference between autonomy and heteronomy is whether the will of the law is determined by itself or by the object of the will: the former is the categorical imperative, and the latter is the hypothetical imperative:

> If the will seeks the law that is to determine it *anywhere else* than in the fitness of its maxims for its own giving of universal law—consequently if, in going beyond itself, it seeks this law in a property of any of its objects—*heteronomy* always results. The will in that case does not give itself the law; instead the object, by means of its relation to the will, gives the law to it. This relation, whether it rests upon inclination or upon representations of reason, lets only hypothetical imperatives become possible: I ought to do something *because I will something else*. On the contrary, the moral and therefore categorical imperative says: I ought to act in such or such a way even though I have not willed anything else. The latter must therefore abstract from all objects to this extent: that they have no *influence* at all on the will, so that practical reason (the will) may not merely administer an interest not belonging to it but may simply show its own commanding authority as supreme lawgiving.[7]

Will itself determines the law of will, so the will shall be tested with its set law for any object it seeks. In this case, the set law has an intrinsic priority over the object desired. If the object of will determines the law of will, the result is that the law formulation depends on the desired object of will instead. Making the law according to the desired object requires a knowledge of the object. Therefore, the so-called heteronomy is actually to set the law based on knowledge of objects. It is in this sense that Mou Zongsan lays the foundation for the distinction between fact and value, knowledge and morality, heteronomy and autonomy. He once clearly claimed that "telling the difference by means of the true and false in knowledge to decide human acts is moral heteronomy."[8] Thus, Mou Zongsan depicts the difference between Gaozi's "external righteousness" and Mencius' "internal righteousness" through the distinction between knowledge and morality, fact and value, in order to clarify that Gaozi's standpoint is heteronomy, while Mencius' is autonomy.

However, from the previous analysis, we know that Mencius' idea that "benevolence and righteousness are all internal" still presents a context with its specific issue, and its connotation is not equal to autonomous morality. Mencius' line of argumentation for "benevolence and righteousness are all internal" is that, just like the virtue of benevolence which has its roots in human nature, so does the virtue of righteousness. Mencius strongly advocates that "benevolence and righteousness are all internal" in order to clarify that the different virtues of benevolence and righteousness both have their root in human nature: this is their common ground. This can be reasonably extended to a universal proposition: anything deserving to be called virtue has its foundation in human nature. Since ethical activities are of different kinds, so are the virtues able to practice and realize those ethical activities. The achievement of a person's virtue, namely, through the cultivation of virtue accomplishing the realization of a person, means essentially that an education in moral virtue is an education to become a realized person. Personality needs some kind of unity, so it will require a certain unity of virtue in order to achieve and realize that personality. In other words, if all kinds of virtues cannot be unified and are even in conflict with each other, it is impossible to create a complete personality. As a result, the diversity of virtues leads to a question that must be answered: how do many different virtues unite? We can argue that, when Mencius asserts that "benevolence and righteousness are all internal" and clarifies the common foundation of different virtues in human nature, this is for the purpose of virtue unity. If he had agreed with Gaozi that "benevolence is internal and righteousness is external," it would have been difficult to defend the unity of virtue.

In fact, we can clearly see Mencius' solution to this problem. "Zisi and Mencius' Wuxing Thought," widely recognized in the history of Confucianism, may be able to explain the unity of virtue. Benevolence, righteousness, propriety, wisdom and sageliness, "the five integrate harmoniously to form virtue": this idea can be found in the chapter "Five Aspects of Conduct" of the texts excavated from Mawangdui and Guodian. This means that Zisi used a refined conception of "five aspects of conduct" to explain the unity of virtue. Benevolence, righteousness, propriety, wisdom and sageliness "are formed within" and for this they can be called "aspects of virtue." The five are formed within and are united in the heart-mind, achieving their "integration and harmony" which can be defined as "virtue." Mencius apparently inherits the idea of Zisi, but he is not satisfied with the interpretation of the unity of virtues directly from the "five aspects of conduct," but rather resorts to the common foundation for the different virtues (that is, human nature) to demonstrate the unity of virtue. Xunzi said that "Zisi provided the tune for them, and Mencius harmonized it," and obviously there is a difference between them.

Intuitively, the error of Mou Zongsan is that he generally interprets benevolence and righteousness as moral laws, and thus he understands "benevolence and righteousness are found within" as autonomous morality. But, in fact, both benevolence and righteousness are not moral laws, but specific moral items. Moral law can presuppose a moral subject able to achieve self-legislation, which can be further analyzed according to two categories: one is the concept of moral subject and the other one is the concept of the rule or the law. If we consider the particular historical period and cultural background of the "moral subject" (in Kant's time, it may be traced back to the ethical beliefs of Protestantism), it is hard for us to recognize a similar concept of "moral subject" in Confucianism. Even if we can analyze the concept of moral subject in Confucianism, it is difficult to recognize the existence of a similar "law" in Confucian thought, and even if we can find a concept matching with the "law" in the long history and development of Confucianism, it will be difficult to see it as the core concept of Confucian ethical thought. Moreover, the Kantian moral subject is quite at odds with the ethics practice advocated in Confucianism. From the Confucian standpoint, the concept of the Kantian moral subject means a theoretical abstraction of self, and the result is the authentic self—needless to say, this is a real and concrete self, recognized in oneself and by others, within ethical human relations, which fails to actually appear in the hidden background of morality. For example, if my honoring my parents means that my authentic self exists, the key is that I do not honor my parents for moral reasons.

Besides, there are a few points in Confucius' and Mencius' reasoning often cited by Mou Zongsan and his successors to prove that the spirit of Confucian ethics is moral autonomy:

The Master said, "Is virtue a remote thing? I wish to be virtuous, and lo! Virtue is at hand."

(*Lunyu* VII.30)

Yan Yuan asked about perfect virtue. The Master said, "To subdue one's self and return to propriety is perfect virtue. If a man can for one day subdue himself and return to propriety, all under heaven will ascribe perfect virtue to him. Is the practice of perfect virtue from a man himself, or is it from others?"

(*Lunyu* XII.1)

Mencius wrote, "[...] Benevolence, righteousness, propriety, and knowledge are not infused into us from without. We are certainly furnished with them. And a different view is simply owing to want of reflection. Hence it is said, 'Seek and you will find them. Neglect and you will lose them.' Men differ from one another in regard to them—some as much again as others, some five times as much, and some to an incalculable amount—it is because they cannot carry out fully their natural powers."

(*Mengzi* VIA.6)

Mencius wrote, "When we get by our seeking and lose by our neglecting—in that case seeking is of use to getting, and the things sought for are those which are in ourselves. When the seeking is according to the proper course, and the getting is only as appointed—in that case the seeking is of no use to getting, and the things sought are without ourselves."

(*Mengzi* VIIA.3)

Though Confucius' statements, "I wish to be virtuous, and lo! Virtue is at hand" and "practice the perfect virtue from oneself," and Mencius' "benevolence is internal" have different focuses, they are basically the same. Confucius tries to show that everyone has the inherent ability to achieve virtue and the will to realize this practice. Mencius clearly ascribes the intrinsic ability to achieve the virtues to human nature, and the will to achieve virtue to the heart-mind ("to the mind belongs the office of thinking. By thinking, it can obtain it, by neglecting to think, it fails to do this"). By comparison, Confucius' idea is more basic and simple while Mencius' analysis adds a further interpretation of Confucius' thought. Moreover, the structure of heart-mind/nature elucidated by Mencius, to a great extent, sets the ground for the discussion of later Confucianism. Following the view of Mou Zongsan, Li Minghui states that the two textual passages quoted from Confucius contain a concept of "autonomy," because only when the moral law is based on the principle of autonomy can it meet the requirement that "ought to be implies be able to."[9] In Kant's theory, we must understand the concept of freedom in order to understand how "ought to be implies be able to." As a being existing with a free and rational will, man has the obligation to comply with self-made law so as to embody human being *qua* human being, and this implies "ought to be." As a being with a free and rational will, man has the capacity to comply with self-made law so as to achieve human being *qua* human being, and this implies "be able to." But a more basic premise of "ought to be implies be able to" is that the human being with rational and free will as its essential feature should first be a being with the ability of self-legislation, so a higher "ability" is here implied. It is this higher "ability" that determines human being *qua* human being and requires a human being to reflect and achieve his essence. Therefore, in Kant's theory, the relationship between "ought to be" and "able to" actually has two aspects: with regard to practical freedom, it is "ought to be implies be able to"; with regard to transcendental freedom, it is "be able to implies ought to be."[10] To be exact, the latter is "the metaphysical basis of morality." And the "ought to be" and "be able to" in practical freedom should take the "be able to" of transcendental freedom as its basis. In this way, Li Minghui's statement above-mentioned could be seen as vain and empty, because this "be able to" is not based on the corresponding "ought to be" of moral laws, but together with the "ought to be" here, they are based on a higher "be able to" in the sense of theory of existence. In other words, the "ought to be" contained in the "be able to implies ought to be" does not necessarily take the form of the moral law, and Kant's direct combination of man's practical ability and the system based on laws shows the particular background of ethical life. Needless to say, a system based on laws has its roots in Jewish-Christian culture but is distant from Confucian culture. Therefore, the key to interpreting "I wish to be virtuous, and lo! Virtue is at hand" and "practice the perfect virtue from oneself" according to moral autonomy, is to explain "I" as a legislator with a free will and "benevolence" as the moral law established by "I."[11]

The saying "seek and you will find them. Neglect and you will lose them" can be found in Books VI and VII of the *Mencius*. In the latter, the exposition is more detailed and complete. According to the context, Mencius compares the "seeking" and "getting" of virtue with that of riches and honor, and his stance is to illustrate the moral virtue foundation of human nature: benevolence, righteousness, propriety and wisdom are inherent in human nature, so seek and you will find them; neglect and you will lose them. Sun Shi's commentary on the passage "seek and you will find them; neglect and you will lose them" in Book VII states that:

> this chapter highlights that benevolence depends on oneself, while wealth and rank are matters of destiny. Mencius advocates that benevolence, righteousness, propriety and wisdom are inherent in human nature. By complying with human nature, you will find them, while to part away from it then makes you to miss them. Benevolence, righteousness, propriety, and wisdom are innate in human nature, existing at the beginning and given to us, it is a nobility conferred by Heaven. When the seeking is according to the proper course, we will cultivate the nobility of Heaven, and the nobility of man derives accordingly. The nobility of Heaven can be cultivated, and yet some do not obtain their nobility, others obtain and lose it. Whether getting or losing, it depends on destiny. In that case, the seeking of nobility of man is of no use to getting and the things sought are without ourselves. Since the nobility of man is not specialized by us, it is something without ourselves.[12]

In the *Treatise on the Summum Bonum*, Mou Zongsan expressed his distinctive textual interpretation of this passage of Book VII.[13] In this regard, I will make a brief analysis.

First, regarding the object of what should be "sought and found," Mou Zongsan holds that "what Mencius implies" includes two categories, i.e., "the original heart-mind (*benxin*) of benevolence, righteousness, propriety and wisdom, and the virtues of benevolence, righteousness, loyalty and honesty that the original heart-mind gives expression to."[14] Broadly speaking, this interpretation is not wrong, but if it is carefully analyzed, it may be problematic. "Benevolence, righteousness, propriety and wisdom" are the four moral sprouts of the heart-mind, but at the same time, they cannot be called "the heart-mind possessing the four moral sprouts." Mencius clearly states that "To the mind belongs the office of thinking. By thinking, it gets the right view of things; by neglecting to think, it fails to do this." That is to say, "seeking" in "seek and you will get" is, specifically, "thinking." If the "heart-mind" controls the function of "thinking," namely, the function of "seeking," according to Mou Zongsan, "the original heart of benevolence, righteousness, propriety and wisdom" is the seeker as well as the object being sought. This interpretation may be truly possible in a metaphysical sense, but it does not entirely comply with the idea of Mencius. Although Mencius discusses both the heart-mind and human nature, the difference between them is clear and significant to him. Denying the difference between the heart-mind and human nature in Mencius' thought would put out of sight the original connotation of Mencius' thought. In fact, what can be sought by the "thinking of the heart-mind" can only be the virtue innate to human nature. Mencius' argumentation is not completely the same as Confucius', but in a sense, the two share the same context. They both point out that virtue is rooted in human nature's innate ability, so the key to realize this virtue lies in the human being himself. The thinking of the heart-mind contributes to "seeking and getting" the virtues of benevolence, righteousness, propriety and wisdom.

Moreover, Mou Zongsan believes that this passage of Mencius is "clearly the same as" what Confucius claimed when he says that "I wish to be virtuous, and lo! Virtue is at hand," but on the contrary, we "cannot say in the same way 'I wish to be rich and honorable, and lo! Riches and honor are at hand.'" In this regard, he quotes Confucius' statement regarding riches and honor: "If the search for riches were sure to be successful, though I should become a groom with whip in hand to get them, I would do so. As the search may not be successful, I will follow after that which I love" (*Lunyu* VII.12).[15] In his interpretation of Confucius' statement, Mou Zongsan also points out that "the search surely being successful" is a "search that is possible and through which something will be obtained," while "the search may not be successful" means "something that we can search for but are not sure to obtain," so it does not mean that it is impossible to search for riches and honor. He means that we might fail to search for them, which is shown in the sentence, "the seeking is of no use to getting."[16] In his interpretation of Mencius' statement "when the seeking is according to the proper course and the getting is only as appointed—in that case the seeking is of no use to getting, and the things sought are without ourselves," Mou Zongsan made a misappropriation of Kant's notion of moral philosophy. He says:

> Such seeking is surely not an inappropriate seeking. Even if the seeking is according to the proper course and one seeks following the proper path and according to the true moral principle, this will not guarantee that he or she can absolutely get what they are seeking, because the moral principle related to the aspect of getting or not getting, according to Kant, is a comprehensive relationship, not an analytical relationship. In Mencius' words, that is 'the getting is only as appointed,' getting or not getting is determined by "fate" (*ming*), which can never be determined by moral principle.[17]

Mou Zongsan further comments that in moral matters,

> what Kant said was completely the same as what Mencius stated, and
> they were perfectly aware of what they asserted. "The things sought for
> are those which are in ourselves" and "the things sought are without our-
> selves" are completely consistent! This shows that wherever the truth lies,
> the mind and the theory are in line with each other. Chinese and Western
> philosophical integration also comes from this.[18]

A similar interpretation is also seen in his translation and annotation of the
Critique of Practical Reason:

> Obeying the moral proverbs (commands) is to obey the moral rules, and
> there is no trick at all. There is no need to give instructions about the
> means and methods in this regard. Order you to obey, and you shall obey.
> If you are willing to do it, you can do it. If you do not want to, there is
> no way to make you do it. This is Confucius' statement "I wish to be vir-
> tuous, and lo! Virtue is at hand." And, it is also what Mencius claimed by
> saying "when we get by our seeking and lose by our neglecting—in that
> case seeking is of use to getting, and the things sought for are those which
> are in ourselves." But it is almost impossible to satisfy the proverbs, which
> is what Mencius calls "things sought are without ourselves."[19]

Within the framework of deontology, Kant distinguishes morality and
happiness according to the division between rationality and sensibility.
Morality corresponds to the existence of human rationality and happiness
corresponds to the existence of sensibility. If it is difficult to determine the
structure of Mencius' thought deontology, it is also difficult to assert that the
"proper course" in "seeking is according to the proper course" is what Kant
calls "moral law." Similarly, if it is difficult to determine whether Kant's distinction between rationality and sensibility corresponds to Mencius' thought,
it is equally difficult to assert whether Kant's distinction between rationality
and sensibility is the same as the distinction between "things sought are in
ourselves" and "things sought are without ourselves" proposed by Mencius.
An evident difference is that Kant ultimately ensures the consistency of morality and happiness through God and the immortal soul, while for Mencius,
the consistency of morality and happiness cannot be guaranteed. The reason
is that the ideas of "morality" and "happiness" are not the same. In other
words, in Mencius, there is neither Kant's idea of morality—"things sought
are in ourselves" does not mean that the moral law has an inner feature of
autonomy, but it means that virtue is rooted in the inherent ability of the
human being; nor is there a Kantian concept of happiness—"things sought
are without ourselves" does not merely refer to the satisfaction of a separated
perception externally achieved, but also to all those factors external to the
man itself.

Carrying on Mou Zongsan's interpretive approach to Kantianism, Li Minghui interprets the difference between "the things sought are without ourselves" and "the things sought for are those which are in ourselves" (Mencius) as the difference between natural causality and causality by freedom (Kant).[20] However, this is a plausible explanation. Causality is a category used to explain the "production" activity. What contributes to the production of something is the reason for the production of the thing. What the reason causes is the result related to the reason. Kant's distinction between natural causality and causality by freedom involves two different levels, which can be regarded as two different types of "production" activities.[21] One is the "production" related to the world of perception, where the reason and the result are set in a fixed chronological sequence, resulting in the reason of one thing being different from the thing as the result of the reason. Such causality is natural causality, which corresponds to the law of nature. The other is the "production" activity in the world of rationality, where the cause and effect relationship does not belong to a chronological sequence, resulting in the reason of one thing and the thing as a result of the reason being united in the existence of the thing. This causality is causality by freedom, which is summarized as transcendental freedom having "absolute spontaneity" in the *Critique of Pure Reason*. The production of any thing has its own nature, which is the core meaning of transcendental freedom, and thus provides the core meaning of causality by freedom. That is to say, the causality relationship between the reason inherent in the thing itself, and the thing itself as the result, is the causality by freedom. What we should pay attention to is that Kant's idea of transcendental freedom is first of all a cosmological concept.[22] For any being in the universe, not only human beings, but also the beings in the natural world, transcendental freedom and causality by freedom understood in this way are effective. In other words, natural causality is related to the being which is the object of knowledge derived by the perception, while causality by freedom is related to the being as the object of rational knowledge. Since one being can be regarded as the perceptual object as well as the rational object, natural causality and causality by freedom can be applied to the same object without contradiction. In this way, we can say that one thing can be produced according to two reasons, as perceptual object and rational object; the former belongs to natural causality and the latter to causality by freedom.[23] When it is implemented explicitly on the peculiar being in this universe, that is, the human being, transcendental freedom can be realized as practical freedom and causality by freedom can be embodied as the autonomy of self-legislation and self-observation. In this moment causality by freedom corresponds to the moral law.

Mencius' distinction between the "the things sought for are those which are in ourselves" and "the things sought are without ourselves" differs from the distinction between natural causality and causality by freedom proposed by Kant. First of all, in Mencius, the distinction pertains to the sphere of human being, and cannot be applied to other objects, while Kant's distinction between natural causality and causality by freedom has a cosmological significance and can either be applied to human beings or to common existents. Secondly, even if it is implemented in the sphere of human being, the statement "the things sought for are those which are in ourselves" is stressed by Mencius to illustrate that moral virtue cultivation must be sought through the thinking of the heart-mind and starting from human nature. Kant used his causality by freedom to illustrate the autonomous root of moral law. The difference between virtue and law makes it impossible for us to see them as identical. Thirdly, "the things sought are without ourselves" does not correspond to Kant's so-called natural causality. In other words, whether men are able to obtain riches and honor is not an issue concerning natural causality. Natural causality emphasizes necessity and the laws of nature, while the "appointed" in "the getting is only as appointed" cannot be considered equal to natural necessity or natural law, or maybe there is just a contingent concept here. Even if necessity is applied in order to eliminate the contingency, it is only a scientific interpretation from a peculiar perspective, and it is hard to say this applies to Mencius' thought.

In fact, through our analysis we can understand the key of Mencius' distinction between "seeking inside" and "seeking outside." First of all, when we use the term "seeking," it indicates that there is a certain distance between "the one who seeks" (求者) and "the thing sought" (所求者). To seek means having not obtained yet "the thing sought." Secondly, only when "the things sought" naturally belong to me can I guarantee that the results of getting or not getting are controlled by my willingness to seek, that is, "seeking is of use to getting", and only when "the things sought" naturally do not belong to me can I say "when the seeking is according to the proper course, and the getting is only as appointed," that is, "the seeking is of no use to getting." Therefore, only for those things which naturally belong to me but I have not obtained yet can I say "when I get by my seeking and lose by my neglecting." Then, what is it that naturally belongs to me but I have not obtained yet? Mencius' answer is obviously the "original nature" that I have not discovered or realized yet, that is, the potential inherent in human nature. Only according to the inner potential of human nature can I say "when I get by my seeking and lose by my neglecting." Here "seeking" and "getting" are properly understood only in the sense of realized potential. Of course, according to Mencius' description, "seeking" here is first the "seeking through the heart-mind," that is "seeking through the thinking ability," and "getting" is "getting through the heart-mind," or, "getting through thinking." The interpretation is not only consistent with the explanation "virtue means to obtain" (德者，得也) but also is correlated to the combined terms of "virtue" and "human nature."

Furthermore, the "seeking through the heart-mind," or "seeking through the thinking ability" here refers to the decision completely controlled by me and closely related to the achievement of virtue, or the choice to select, which is the "selection" claimed by Confucius in his statement "I will select their good qualities and follow them, their bad qualities and avoid them." When

Mencius says that benevolence and righteousness are within human nature, he does not mean that benevolence and righteousness exist in human nature as a ready-made thing and the seeking for benevolence and righteousness seems to take up a ready-made thing, but this means that man's intrinsic ability received from Heaven ("what Heaven has conferred is called 'nature'") is the basis to achieve the virtue of benevolence and righteousness. So, the key is whether man is willing to and is able to bring out the inherent ability received from Heaven, so as to achieve the virtue of benevolence and righteousness. As for the intention to carry out this conduct and realize this virtue, as long as one is willing to, he can do it. Therefore, there is an inherent choice about the self itself. This choice or decision is different from the choice related to external things. For example, for my choice to buy a specific brand of refrigerator, the result is that I have a refrigerator of that specific brand. It is a matter of choice towards an object, which has nothing to do with self itself. However, the inherent choice concerning virtue is different, because it reveals the inner self, or we can say, gives realization to the self. The result is that the manifestation of the self is performed uniquely. Plainly said, how I make my choice, this decides the person I am. Since what I obtain and what I lose from this choice not only depend on what I "seek" or "neglect" ("when we get by our seeking and lose by our neglecting"), but also concern the manifestation of the self, so this choice is internal and inherent. Because different inherent choices reveal different selves, this leads to different results. So, it is in this sense that this choice is also a kind of "seeking," and also has "what it seeks" and "what it obtains." The inherent unity between "seeking" and "obtaining" is based on the existential process of human beings, that is to say, there is no other result outside the existence of human beings.

In order to truly understand the inherent ability related to the choice concerning the achievement of virtue, one must distinguish the inherent choice's "seeking" from desire's "seeking" and hope's "seeking" in the general sense. First of all, the desire's "seeking" exists in human beings as well as in animals and corresponds to sensory ability, such as for beauty and delicacy. Generally speaking, it is the appetitive desire described by Mencius in the textual passage "for the mouth to desire sweet tastes, the eye to desire beautiful colors, the ear to desire pleasant sounds, the nose to desire fragrant odors, and the four limbs to desire ease and rest—these things are natural." We know that, as far as the "seeking" related to the choice is concerned, we rely on the mind (heart-mind), that is, "to the mind belongs the office of thinking." Secondly, in the "seeking" related to hope, the object sought may be impossible, such as immortality, but still something we can hope for. However, we cannot choose immortality, that is to say, the object sought in the "seeking" of choice must be within the range of ability.[24] Specifically, when it comes to the inherent choice concerning the achievement of virtue and self-realization, what to be sought is the innate ability of the self. Besides, in Chinese, "seeking" not only refers to the inner search or desire but also refers to the method of this seeking process. In this regard, in terms of the inner desire's intention, the "seeking" inherent to the choice, desire's "seeking" and hope's "seeking" appear to be similar, but their difference depends on what is to be sought in the "seeking" inherent to choice, since what seeks is the inner heart-mind, so what is sought is the innate ability of human nature. As a result, seek something and you will obtain it. The desired behavior itself does not seek other results different from this behavior itself. Although in hope's "seeking" or desire's "seeking" what seeks is still internal to the self (the former includes the mouth, eyes, ears and nose, and the latter may be the intention or the will), the thing sought is not inherent in ourselves. Therefore, the appetitive behavior itself cannot guarantee that the desire can be satisfied. For example, the satisfaction of sexual desire and immortality are not within the seeker's innate ability. So, we can divide the three ways of "seeking" into two categories, inner seeking and external seeking, or seeking in oneself and seeking from outside. Of course, the latter is what Mencius refers to by saying "when the seeking is according to the proper course, and the getting is only as appointed," and the former is what Mencius means by saying "we get by our seeking and lose by our neglecting," or what Confucius means with "I wish to be virtuous, and lo! Virtue is at hand." Such particular internal seeking is, in fact, a person's inherent requirement to himself for self-realization, and the inner intention of the human being is to achieve what he can achieve. This implies an understanding of the noble nature of the human being, and also implies the concept of a noble self.[25] For the "seeking from outside" of "when the seeking is according to the proper course, and the getting is only as appointed," it is merely inferior to what a man is and what he realizes and accomplishes, in other words, inferior to the existence of human beings. Riches and honor can undoubtedly be desired, that is to say, they can be hoped for, but riches and honor do not belong to the inner self. Therefore, whether we can obtain riches and honor lies only in our destiny. No matter whether we can obtain riches and honor or not, this has nothing to do with what the self is, and it has no connection with a noble self possessing his fate.

So, when it comes to "as long as you want, you can," what is the difference from Kant's statement that "you can do whatever your intention decides"? It seems that we could interpret Kant's freedom of will as freedom of internal choice, and understand Mencius' "to the mind belongs to the office of thinking. By thinking, it gets the right view of things, and by neglecting to think, it fails to do this" as something similar to Kant's freedom of will. However, Mencius connects the freedom of choice with virtue and only discusses freedom of choice in relation to the will to act, which is ultimately the basis to achieve human virtue and thus makes the human being complete and realized. Kant instead connects freedom of will with the moral law, talking about freedom of will by directly pointing to behavior itself. The connotation and the respective theoretical frameworks are not the same. For Mencius, the human being is born with the innate ability to achieve virtue, which is first shown in the ability of internal choice. Although the right choices and the intention to act correctly are the keys to achieving the virtues of benevolence and righteousness, they are only the starting point, and there should be a continuous cultivation process for the completion of virtue. In Kant, the freedom of will as "a rational fact" must be realized according to the moral law, or as Kant says, "freedom is the reason of the existence of moral law, and moral law is the reason of the cognition of freedom."[26] In this regard, the aim of freedom of will, first of all, is not to achieve virtue, but to achieve the moral law. Besides, the relationship between freedom of will and moral law is analytical, without a process beginning from the freedom of will and ending at the moral law: there is only a kind of inquiry or examination, but no cultivation.

Notes

1 Mou Zongsan, *Treatise on the Summum Bonum* (Student Book Store, 1985), p. 19.
2 Li Minghui, *Confucianism and Kant* (Linking Publishing, 1990), p. 12.
3 Mou Zongsan, *Treatise on the Summum Bonum*, p. 14.
4 Mou Zongsan, *Treatise on the Summum Bonum*, p. 15.
5 Mou Zongsan, *Treatise on the Summum Bonum*, p. 15.
6 Mou Zongsan, *Treatise on the Summum Bonum*, p.18.
7 Immanuel Kant, *Groundwork of the Metaphysics of Morals*, 4:441, trans. and ed. by Mary. J. Gregor (Cambridge University Press, 1996), pp. 89–90. The translation refers to the translation version of Mou Zongsan, Miao Litian and Tang Yue.
8 Mou Zongsan, *The Substance of Mind and the Substance of Nature*, Vol. 3 (Shanghai Ancient Books, 1999), p. 361.
9 Li Minghui, *Confucianism and Kant*, pp. 35–36.
10 For the distinction and connection between practical freedom and transcendental freedom in Kant's thought, see Martin Heidegger, *The Essence of Human Freedom: An Introduction to Philosophy*, trans. by Ted Sadler (Continuum, 2002).
11 We cannot deny that Mou Zongsan pays no attention to the inappropriateness of interpreting "benevolence" as a common law, but he fails to realize the serious consequences of such rough interpretation. For example, he said:

> The benevolence advocated by Confucius is based on his specific, clear, sincere concern in his mind, and in real life, he makes specific and messy guidance and inspiration. We cannot say that in this context hides no connotation of benevolence as moral rationality, or the common rule of morality, and also we cannot say that this mixed universal law is not transcendental, and it's not effective for all "rational existence." However, Confucius does not make an abstract reverse display by means of transcendental analysis, but only displays it in specific, clear, sincere and sad real life. Therefore, the common law of benevolence is not the common law abstractly suspended, but it is the common mixed in sincere and sad real life to be the specific common, which will spare no efforts to nurture everything like the free-flowing mercury, or the running ball in a plate as life is in hardship Its transcendental nature and transcendence are not the transcendental nature suspended there lonely, but the inherent transcendence and concrete transcendence mixed in real life.
> (Mou Zongsan, *Substance of Mind and the Substance of Nature*, Vol. 1, p. 100)

It's surely true to hold that "Confucius' 'benevolence' is implemented in specific, real life"; however, this opinion is stressed by Mou Zongsan not to show that Kant's deontology and Confucianism are fundamentally different, but to prove that Confucianism goes further than Kant, not only establishing a transcendental basis and objective ground of moral law based on metaphysical height (*dao* body and nature noumenon), but also establishing the subjective basis of moral laws (mind noumenon) at the metaphysical level. In other words, his logic is still Kantian: first of all, it is the moral law, and then, the real implementation of the moral law in the mind.

12 See *Notes and Commentaries on Mencius*, Vol. 2 (Zhonghua Book Company, 1980), p. 2764.

13 Mou Zongsan, *Treatise on the Summum Bonum*, p. 146.

14 Mou Zongsan, *Treatise on the Summum Bonum*, p. 147.

15 Another passage discussing riches and honor reads: "Riches and honors are what men desire. If they cannot be obtained in the proper way, they should not be held. Poverty and meanness are what men dislike. If they cannot be avoided in the proper way, they should not be avoided" (*Lunyu* IV.5).

16 Mou Zongsan, *Treatise on the Summum Bonum*, p. 147

17 Mou Zongsan, *Treatise on the Summum Bonum*, p. 148.

18 Mou Zongsan, *Treatise on the Summum Bonum*, p. 149.

19 See *Kant's Moral Philosophy*, trans. and annotated by Mou Zongsan (Student Book Store, 1983), p. 178. The part of Kant's text that this translation refers to is about the difference between moral command and the rule of happiness:

> As for the categorical moral imperative, each human being's ability can accept it in any circumstance. As for the rule of happiness under the condition of the experience, only a few can endure it: even just based on the single intention, it is far from what the individual ability can achieve. The reason is, as for the categorical imperative, it can only rely on the fact that the certainty is a true and pure standard, but in the case of the rule of happiness, it depends on carrying out the natural strength and ability to achieve the desired object. Such a command, i.e., "every man should pursue his own happiness," sounds quite foolish because people cannot order someone to do something that this someone cannot help but want to do. People giving this command should only provide someone with regulations or strategies, because he cannot do whatever he wants to. However, it is reasonable to give a moral command in the name of the obligation. First, the reason is that, if the moral rule conflicts with desires and interests, not everyone is willing to obey it. Secondly, regarding how someone can apply the strategies to follow this rule, it needs no instruction: in such a relationship, he can do whatever he wishes. In the Confucian thought, we can find the saying: "Shall you be seeking for much happiness."

Confucianism has such sayings as "seeking for more happiness by oneself." The text corresponding to the annotation involves the difference between the moral imperative and happiness rules: "for the moral categorical imperative, each person's ability."

20 Li Minghui, *Confucianism and Kant*, p. 36.

21 Immanuel Kant, *Critique of Practical Reason*, 5:94, trans. by Han Shuifa (Commercial Press, 1999), p. 102 et seq.

22 Immanuel Kant, *Critique of Pure Reason*, A445/B473, trans. by Deng Xiaomang, ed. by Yang Zutao (People's Publishing House, 2004), p. 374 et seq.

23 From a historical perspective, we can say that Kant's peculiar understanding of necessity and causality by freedom has an ancient predecessor. Let's look at Aristotle's distinction between production and practice. The purpose of production is the product outside of the production activities themselves, and what corresponds to them is the technical wisdom, while the purpose of practice is practice itself, and what corresponds to it is the practical wisdom. Aristotle distinguishes production and practice through the concept of "purpose," while Kant uses the concept of causality to distinguish natural necessity and necessity by freedom. Considering the variable features of nature with a scientific attitude is actually to understand nature from the perspective of technique (*techne*), or rather, to understand nature from the perspective of production. It is by no means accidental that the ancient Greeks regarded nature as the highest "technique." Therefore, the distinction proposed by Kant between natural necessity and necessity by freedom obviously corresponds to Aristotle's distinction between production and practice, though Aristotle does not distinguish the perceptual object and the rational object as Kant did. At least, they show some consistency in the understanding of the unique nature of practice. Practice as man's activity, from the perspective of purpose, has no other purposes out of himself; from the perspective of causality, there is no other external reason except the practitioner's will.

24 The crucial point for choice lies in action or inaction, rather than being able to or unable to. Mencius once made a clear distinction between the two:

> "How may the difference between the not doing a thing, and the not being able to do it, be represented?" "In such a thing as taking the Tai mountain under your arm, and leaping over the north sea with it, if you say to people 'I am not able to do it,' that is a real case of not being able. In such a matter as breaking off a branch from a tree at the order of a superior, if you say to people 'I am not able to do it,' that is a case of not doing it, it is not a case of not being able to do it."
>
> (*Mengzi* IA.7)

25 We can find many aspects of Mencius' understandings of the nobility of man, such as his distinction between the nobility of Heaven and the nobility of man. The most crucial point is that man is noble due to the intrinsic nature received from Heaven.

26 Kant, *Critique of Practical Reason*, trans. by Han Shuifa, Preface, p. 2, footnote.

8   Confucian ethics

Virtue-based or law-based?

The concept of autonomy is related to Kant's fundamental understanding of morality, and it is a pivotal concept which exerts a crucial influence within Kant's moral philosophy. Considering the peculiar historical context related to the thought of moral autonomy, explaining early Confucian ethical thought—including Mencius'—with the autonomy concept not only leads to some problems in understanding, it will also lead to a significant alteration of the whole connotation. We could say that, through the remolded Kantianism carried out by Mou Zongsan, early Confucian ethical thought is almost unrecognizable.

As is well known, Kant's moral philosophy focused on the core concept of autonomy is a model of deontology, and self-legislation is the main connotation of autonomy. Therefore, behind autonomous morality there is actually a legalist thought. In other words, the law concept becomes the dominant concept of this ethical thought. It must be pointed out that the reason why Kant adopted a legalist viewpoint in moral issues is that he understood freedom through the causality category, and thus he put forward the concepts of moral law and moral autonomy based on the law concept implied from the category of causality. Furthermore, the ideological origin of Kantian moral legalism can be found in Judeo-Christian religious legalism. On Kant's moral philosophy, MacIntyre once pointed out that the moral judgment of modern deontology is just "the ghost of the concept of the divine law."[1] According to the Old Testament, Moses' Ten Commandments are the divine law bestowed by God on the Jews, as well as God's divine command or divine providence. According to the New Testament, Jesus' Sermon on the Mount is not meant to destroy the law but to fulfill the law. Therefore, the Sermon on the Mount is widely known as "the law of love." Regarding obedience to the order or the law of God as a moral theory, this is the so-called Divine Command Theory. In this sense, as a Puritan believer, Kant's adoption of the concept of the law to interpret morality and nature (moral law and natural law) is by no means accidental. In particular, the categorical imperative Kant proposed appears to be a moral order made by man as a rational being, but is actually a modern transformation of the Divine Command Theory, even though in the construction of his deontology Kant clearly criticizes the Divine Command Theory and rules it out of morality.[2] Behind autonomous morality there is in fact a theonomous morality. When a believer has engraved the sacred divine law in his mind, this means that he can reveal his good inner conscience: the law has been internalized, even if the authority of this law comes from outside, i.e., has an external source. In this case, if we consider the source of law, it is heteronomy; from the perspective of the motivation to abide by the law, it is autonomy. Therefore, Hegel clearly connects Kant's moral philosophy and the Jewish spirit based on Mosaic Law and compares it with Jesus' Sermon on the Mount. When it comes to the difference between pious believers and practitioners of Kantian religious autonomy, he directly states:

> It does not lie in that the former converts those to be a slave while the latter preserve their freedom, but lies in that the owners of the former are out of themselves, while the owners of the latter are within themselves, and at the same time, they are still the slaves of themselves.[3]

Hegel's statement reveals the truth of autonomy. Also, we can see that theologians like Paul Tillich standing on the ground of Christianity greatly criticize autonomous morality and put forward the concept of "theonomy," which is regarded as the unity of autonomy and heteronomy.[4] Meanwhile, as a Jew, Emmanuel Levinas is especially opposed to Kant's idea, and claims that morality means heteronomy, absolute heteronomy.[5] If morality based on an imperative claims that there must be a command issuer, Kant's moral proposition regarding the categorical imperative is incomplete, just as Anscombe later criticizes.[6]

After clarifying the original relationship between Kant's moral philosophy and the Judeo-Christian law doctrine, we can understand why Kant regards law-oriented deontology as the nature of morality. Then, since we all know that in Confucian thought, the concept of "virtue" is far more important than the concept of "law," is it appropriate to evaluate Confucian ethics according to the standard of deontology? Is the fundamental nature of Confucian ethical thought law-oriented deontology or virtue-oriented ethics? As for the fundamental difference between deontology and virtue ethics, let us discuss this from the following three aspects.[7]

First, like utilitarianism, deontology gives more concern to action than to man as the actor of behavior. On the contrary, virtue ethics is more concerned with the actor, man, than the action. In other words, the former focuses on acting by rules, and the latter focuses on instruction in being a human being. The former focuses on whether a behavior is proper or improper and the latter pays attention to beauty or ugliness of personality. Let us look closely at Kant's discussion on universal moral law: "Act like this, which will make the rule of your will be regarded as a principle of the universal legislation at any time."[8] What is directly claimed here is the criterion of action, and on the concept of the criterion Kant says that it is "the subjective principle of action" and "a principle grounded on the action of the subject."[9] This shows that Kant's deontology thought is directed to the action rather than the actor. In Confucian ethical thought, the core idea is the *chengren* (the "complete person"). The so-called "complete person" indicates the moral and virtuous achievement of a perfect personality:

> The Master said, "Suppose a man with the knowledge of Zang Wu Zhong, the freedom from covetousness of Gong Chuo, the bravery of Zhuang of Bian, and the varied talents of Ran Qiu; add to these the accomplishments of the rules of propriety and music—such a one might be reckoned a COMPLETE man." He then added, "But what is the necessity for a complete man of the present day to have all these things? The man, who in the view of gain, thinks of righteousness; who in the view of danger is prepared to give up his life; and who does not forget an old agreement however far back it extends—such a man may be reckoned a COMPLETE man."
>
> (*Lunyu* XIV.12)

Here, "complete person" is generally interpreted as a "perfected person" or "a person with perfect personality," generally referring to the so-called goal of a "complete person" (a man's achievement and perfection). From Confucius' answer we can see that the "complete person" is the primary goal of Confucian ethics and the strategy is the cultivation of virtue. In other words, the education for a "complete person" is an education in moral virtue (*chengde*, 成德). Therefore, Confucian ethical thought should be attributed to virtue ethics rather than deontology.

There is, however, still a need to consider another interpretation that can be attributed to existentialism. We have already mentioned that Kant understands the concept of practice through the causality category and stresses the importance of practitioners' free will on practice. That is, there are no other external reasons except the practitioner's will. This, to a certain extent, is similar to Aristotle's emphasis on the inner purpose of practice: unlike the production activity aiming to produce other things, practice has no other purposes out of the self. Such similarity, by no means accidental, inevitably forces us to regard such a view as seemingly reasonable in many respects: the existence of man is the same with man's action, and only through man's action we can understand "what is man."[10] If you want to answer the question "what is man?" you can only get it by means of the investigation and analysis of the action of man. Thus, it is a difficult problem to distinguish between deontology and virtue ethics by paying more attention to man's action or more to man's existence. However, there is still something plausible in equating man's existence with man's action, which is yet to be further clarified, even if the "existence" is reasonably interpreted as a verb. If the action is appropriately analyzed, time must be understood as the essential condition, because the action is situated in the "time" framework, done in the present of "the moment." When we look at "existence" as a verb, we are able to understand man's existence in the same way and thus say the same words: if we appropriately analyze the existence of *man*, time must be understood as the essential condition because the action of *man* is always situated in the "time" framework, done in the present of "the moment." However, the difference is, when a man makes a commitment to the integrity of himself, his existence is *singular* ("being"), and the process of being requires a continuity, which constitutes the integrity of man, answering the core problem pointing to man's being, "who am I?" In contrast, the action of man is *plural* ("actions"), which can be used to refer to the segment of man's being and the situation of man's being, as well as the whole of man's being. Therefore, if we understand the sentence "man's being is the same with man's actions" as "all of a man's actions constitute his existence," this is probably not wrong. The problem is that the single analysis of human actions and the overall analysis of man's being are not the same. In the analysis of man's actions, the antecedents and consequences of the action itself need to be considered; in the analysis of man's being, we must consider the whole of the being connecting many actions. In other words, even if we pick out more general "event" concepts as the class concepts governing man's actions and man's being and regard man's being as a single event, the two can only be regarded as different types of events.

Therefore, although human action can embody man's being, and man's being is closely related to human action, it is rather inappropriate completely equating man's being to human action, and at least involves some suspicious tendency of reductionism, or is even totally wrong. This means that the distinction made between human action and man's being is effective, and man's being cannot be simply reduced to human action, that is to say, the first distinction between virtue ethics and deontology is effective. We will also clearly answer two influential viewpoints related to reductionism. One is from Heidegger. From the perspective of phenomenology, Heidegger understands time as the essential condition for being, so he regards human action as the same as man's being. The temporality analysis of man's being is called the "ontology of Dasein," or the fundamental ontology, and Heidegger does not oppose interpreting the ontology as "originary ethics." He then puts forward a criticism of Aristotle's ethics, holding that the latter adheres to the metaphysical thinking invented by the Greeks and fails to reach the height of phenomenology, although it is from Aristotle's *Nicomachean Ethics* that he discovers the "signs of hermeneutics."[11] Though the analysis of Dasein's temporality takes into account the wholeness of the self (for this, Heidegger is appealing to man's fear of death and what man "has been"), we cannot equate it to the problem of man's being. This is because the analysis of Dasein's temporality focuses on the present, which is basically a sort of "what it is at present"—in other words, to grasp man's being from man's being-at-present; but we may still insist that man's real life should be a relatively prolonged planning process, in which the future, present and past are closely related. In other words, man's being should be understood as a process of living from birth to death. Therefore, a true present can reflect man's being, but any analysis related to the present still cannot replace the analysis of man as a *process* of being. From an ethical point of view, the most obvious flaw of Heidegger's reductionism is that it cannot talk about self-cultivation. Any present is just a present, while self-cultivation must involve continuity to pursue the boundless progress of virtue. Therefore, the analysis of man's being-at-present (i.e., the analysis of Dasein's temporality) fails to disclose the theme of self-cultivation. It can be seen that Heidegger's idea of time still has the instant-mark flaw, which makes time an instant, and the essence is still to understand time through a mathematical point, although it may be a dynamic and self-discrete moving point where past and future also flash. Related to this, another defect of this reductionism is that from the perspective of ethics, virtue is a stable quality, which can never be affected by the analysis of man's being-at-present. Therefore, when we see Heidegger introducing the dimension of temporality to explain Aristotle's concept of "virtue" as "true and fully expanded possibility of *aletheuein*,"[12] on the one hand, we have to praise his insight, and on the other hand, we should also be aware of the distance between the interpretation of phenomenology and the understanding of ethics.

There is another viewpoint that appears in the field of ethics and is, by consequence, quite well known in the academic world. Strongly influenced by Nietzsche, Bernard Williams puts forward a criticism of all "ethical theories," which he has called "the anti-theoretical nature in ethics."

In his view of ethical issues, if an actual living man's ethics adhere to the specific historical and cultural situation, he calls them "ethical thought." If they is constructed from the abstract philosophical standpoint of philosophers, he calls them "ethical theory." In short, ethical theory corresponds to the theoretical tendency in ethical inquiry, which is a theoretical attempt to explain and construct the ethical ideas of humans by abstract philosophy. Williams summarizes that the essential characteristic of all ethical theories is to construct universal and impartial moral principles as the basis to test and derive specific moral judgment standards. This process shows an evident deductive feature, that is, taking basic ethical principles as a prerequisite to apply in real ethical affairs and obtain a specific moral judgment through practical syllogistic moral reasoning. Williams believes that the abstractness of philosophy determines that the ethical theory constructed by philosophy must rid itself of the real life of man, so the position of philosophy will reinforce many obstacles to our ethical thinking. This is where the meaning lies when he describes his most important work as marking "the limitations of ethics and philosophy": "I want to say, we can have ethical Reflection in a variety of ways—unless our historical and cultural situation makes it impossible, but rarely can philosophy decide how we carry out the ethical thinking."[13] Williams' range of criticism is quite broad. In his argumentation, he not only refers to Kant's moral metaphysics theory, the moral theory of contractualism (he takes Thomas M. Scanlon as an example) and the functionalism theory of John Stuart Mill and others, but also refers to meta-ethics, beginning with G.E. Moore. He even criticizes Aristotle's ethics because, after all, teleological thinking and a metaphysical biological theory occupy an important position in Aristotle's ethics.[14] Therefore, if Williams "mostly agrees with" Aristotle's ethics (as stated by Martha Nussbaum), Williams' criticism is a double-edged sword which will, in turn, damage his own position. If Williams' position goes further and he completely abandons Aristotle's teleology and metaphysical biology, he can only, like Heidegger did, resort to historicism or more thorough contextualism, where everything is remitted to the effective historical-cultural situation, or even to the real-state moment.t.[15] In order to distinguish this historicism from nihilism, one must defend historical rationality.[16] Of course, within Heidegger's thought, the defense of historical rationality does not need to resort to demonstration; instead, it is directly taken for granted or explained with phenomenological terms; man's being is historical, which can only be interpreted as the facticity of man's life.[17] In summary, Williams' anti-theoretical tendency is too extreme. If we follow its thinking consistently, we cannot keep the unity and integrity of man's life. Thus, the stable foundation of a man's life will be removed, and so will the stable foundation where the achievement of virtue lies.

Secondly, the fundamental difference between deontology and virtue ethics can be seen in the difference in essential terminology. The essential terminology of deontology consists of "just" and "unjust," "duty" and "obligation," while the essential terms of virtue ethics are "good" and "evil," "virtuous" and "unvirtuous." This distinction does not mean that the terms of the two ethical paths are limited to the choice of either this or that. In the framework of deontology, of course, there is also the position of virtue, but here virtue can be appropriately illustrated through duty or obligation. For example, Kant defines virtue as "the standard power for the exertion of one's obligation" or "self-discipline consistent with the principles of internal freedom."[18] Since the concept of obligation is regarded as the fundamental concept of ethics, and virtue is still a valid concept but not the essential idea of ethics, virtue must be related to the basic concept of obligation to obtain a reasonable explanation. A man of virtue is a man of good conduct, a man who can do his duty. Similarly, in the ideological framework of virtue ethics, there is also the position of right or obligation, but here obligation must be appropriately illustrated through virtue. Those who advocate virtue ethics believe that behavior legitimacy does not derive from some kind of law, but from the one who practices virtue. A man of virtue can naturally behave properly and naturally be able to know how to do his duty. This is because the concept of virtue, or the corresponding goodness, is regarded as the essential concept of ethics. Therefore, although "right" or "obligation" are still valid concepts, they must be related to virtue or goodness to obtain a reasonable explanation. We know that Kant has cited some examples when explaining the moral law as categorical imperative. For example, he believes that "do not lie" is a moral law that meets the requirements of rationality. However, Confucius describes those who "are determined to be sincere in what they say, and to carry out what they do" as "obstinate little men," which makes him hesitate even to put them in the class below that of the scholars (*Lunyu* XIII.20), and Mencius further explains positively, "The great man does not think beforehand of his words that they may be sincere, nor of his actions that they may be resolute – he simply speaks and does what is right" (*Mengzi* IVB.39). These two behaviors constitute a sharp contrast. In particular, it can be seen from the words of Mencius that if Confucian righteousness is understood as a general principle of law, it is rather distorted. Confucian ethics is virtue ethics centered on the accomplishment of a "complete person," which is far different from Kantian deontology. If we further connect the "do not lie" moral law with Moses' Ten Commandments (the ninth) of the Judeo-Christian tradition, the difference is much clearer. It is rather significant to take telling the truth to the height of a command of God. In Confucian ethics, what is first emphasized is "sincerity in the intercourse with friends." That is, the special virtue of "sincerity" is directed to the relationship with friends. In addition, we can claim that honesty is a virtue for a man as being a man. However, whether for the relationship with friends or the essence of man as human being, "sincerity" here is a virtue which requires consideration according to what one is and the actual situation, and is different from the universal order, whether it is the universal order derived from rationality in Kant's moral philosophy or the universal order due to God's command in Judeo-Christian thought.

Kang Youwei proposed a famous argument in the process of transforming Confucianism into New Confucianism. He believes that the chapter "The Conduct of the Scholar" in the *Book of Rites* has been redacted by Confucius for Confucians, and nearly equates to the Buddhist Commandments or Christian Ten Commandments.[19] Even if we accept that Confucians should act in accordance with the teachings of Confucius described in "The Conduct of the Scholar," such analogy is still inappropriate. "The Conduct of the Scholar" reports the context when Confucius answers the question raised by Duke Ai of Lu about the scholar's behavior, which is named "Seventeen Features of Confucius Explaining Scholars' Conduct" by Kong Yingda. But if we look at the specific content of the seventeen features it is easy to distinguish it from the precepts or commandments. Confucius in this chapter does not point out what Confucians shall abide by, but taking account of real life, he describes the personality pattern of a "great man" for Confucians, including self-reliance, appearance, preparations and precautions, close association with others, solitary course, boldness and determination, becoming an official, anxiety, largeness and generosity, promoting the employment of the worthy and bringing forward the able, employment and promotion of valuable friends, rules and conduct, friendship relations, honor and humility, and other contents related to morality. The "Seventeen" repeatedly says "the scholar has": what the scholar has can only be virtue. Therefore, the "act" here means conduct and virtue, aimed at Confucians' personality accomplishment and positive cultivation, which is totally different from the Buddhist or Christian precepts and commandments. Chen Lai commented on "the teachings about the five regular relations" ("The righteousness of a father, the compassion of a mother, the fraternal kindness of an elder brother, the respect of a younger brother, the filial piety of a son") in *Zuo's Commentary or Zuo's Annals*, stating that "if in the era of Shun the five teachings were issued, their cultural meaning is no lower than Moses' Ten Commandments."[20] This evaluation also places Confucianism in a comparative perspective with Judeo-Christian religion, but we should be careful in our description. In fact, Matteo Ricci noticed that the Confucian religious character was different from that of Christianity: "Although these scholars named Confucians do acknowledge that there is a supreme deity," "there is not any evidence on […] the precepts that must be followed, or any authority to explain or promulgate canons and punish violations against the Supreme being."[21]

Thirdly, the explanation of behavior motivation related to moral life is widely different in deontology and virtue ethics. The former argues that the motivation for moral behavior depends on following an obligation, i.e., a sense of duty. In contrast, the latter argues that the motivation of the action lies in the desire or the purpose closely related to the practitioner himself. Kant points out that respect for the moral law is the key to understanding obligation: "the so-called obligations mean the necessity of action out of respect for moral law."[22] Respect for the moral law is fundamentally respect for the legislator, i.e., man as a rational being, as well as an end (the citizen destined for the kingdom of God). Therefore, the respect here is entirely rational, voluntary, without any fear or force from external objects. It is obvious, however, that it is easy for us to think of the connection between the reverence for rationality and the fear for religion. Kant transforms reverence towards God within Judeo-Christian thought into respect for moral law. Namely, there is atransformation from the heteronomous commandments into the moral autonomy we have discussed. The original legislator is God and now the legislator has become the rational human being himself. The core content of this transformation is, of course, to remove the irrational component of "fear" and what remains is the "respect" that can be explained through rationality. At this point, early Confucianism certainly maintains a distinct "fear": "There are three things of which the superior man stands in awe. He stands in awe of the ordinances of Heaven. He stands in awe of great men. He stands in awe of the words of sages" (*Lunyu* XVI.5). But the greater difference is that the reverence in Confucianism does not show in compliance to divine commandments. The Confucian reverence related to fate granted by Heaven differs from the reverence towards God in Judeo-Christian thought in both form and content.[23] Even the successors of Confucianism transformed "reverence" into "respect" based on a new conception; they could not and should not resort to respect for the moral law as Kant did.

In contemporary Western (i.e., British and American) academic circles, some scholars advocating the revival of traditional virtue ethics put forward sharp criticisms of the existing problems of modern moral philosophy, including the ethical behavior motivation in deontology. In his article "The

Schizophrenia of Modern Ethical Theories," Michael Stocker directly addresses the motivation of ethical behavior. In the first lines of his article, he says that modern ethical theory only focuses on the explanation and demonstration of moral reasons but lacks a review of the motivation in ethical life and the structure of this motivation. He calls the serious disconnection between reason and motivation and the resulting great disharmony "The Schizophrenia of Modern Ethical Theories." He designed a case to illustrate this point from the practical ethical life:

> Suppose you are in a hospital, recovering from a long illness. You are very bored and restless and at loose ends when Smith comes in once again. You are now convinced more than ever that he is a fine fellow and a real friend—taking so much time to cheer you up, travelling all the way across town, and so on. You are very effusive with your praise and thanks that he protests that he always tries to do what he thinks is his duty, what he thinks will be best. You at first think he is engaging in a polite form of self-deprecation, relieving the moral burden. But the more you two speak, the more clear it becomes that he was telling the literal truth: that is not essentially because of you that he come to see you, not because you are friends, but because he thought it his duty, perhaps as a fellow Christian or Communist or whatever, or simply because he knows of no one more in need of cheering up and no one easier to cheer up.[24]

We can further imagine how frustrated you will be after knowing the motivation of Smith coming to see you in hospital. You hope that a friend comes to see you because he thinks you two are good friends or because you have a deep friendship which affects your mutual existence, rather than because of abstract moral obligation as a human being. The motivation is subjective, and the reason is objective, which should be coordinated and consistent. The serious disconnection between reason and motivation will be ultimately caused by reason, that is to say, as long as we can categorically confirm that a certain motivation is worth preserving, it must be the reason that is wrong. In other words, when a practical rationality providing moral reason is far away from our good feelings, in order to protect our ethical life we have reasons to oppose it. In fact, this case does not need to be further analyzed. It is easy to see that if we all were like Smith, who acts entirely out of duty in a cold manner, then we would live in a world absolutely unacceptable. Perhaps the Kingdom mentioned by Kant is such a ruthless world with morals but no friendliness. I believe that most people are not willing to live in it, because that morality not only does not engage our true beings, but even alienates our sincere feelings.

Williams has cited another slightly different case. Imagine that a man is facing an ethical decision: to save a stranger or to save his wife. At that moment he thinks that saving his wife can be justified properly, that is to say, as a moral choice sustained by reason. However,

It might have been hoped by some (for instance, by his wife) that his motivating thought, fully spelled out, would be the thought that it was his wife, not that it was his wife and that in situations of this kind it is permissible to save one's wife.[25]

If the motivation for saving one's wife can only be legitimately defended when there is proper moral permission, it is difficult to accept it as satisfactory. At least, this cannot make the wife satisfied with it. This also shows that universal moral motivation is entirely at odds with our actual ethical life.

Regarding the motivation of ethical behavior, Confucianism can only be understood as virtue ethics. To grasp the motivation within Confucianism, we should first consider *qing* ("feeling, emotion"). The beauty of nature endowed on man is expressed in likes and dislikes, which is the so-called temperament. However, for common people, unlike the Sages, such likes and dislikes derived from nature do not happen overnight but require a long process of learning and cultivation. Even Confucius had to say that although he "had his mind bent on learning" since he was 15, it was not until the age of 70 that he could "follow what my heart desired, without transgressing what was right" (*Lunyu* II.4). This learning process is of course the self-cultivation of moral virtue. Therefore, in terms of the intrinsic effect of transforming and making people complete in their nature, virtue is reflected through a stable temperament.[26] On this basis, we can understand why Confucius claims that, "it is only the (truly) virtuous man, who can love, or who can hate, others" (*Lunyu* IV.3). Confucianism is often said to be a kind of learning that can change and cultivate our temperament: this is an extraordinary theory.

In ethical life, man's behavior motivation is reflected through his nature and emotions, and thus can be revealed through his moral virtue: this is the essence of Confucian ethics. Take the most important virtue as an example, benevolence. From the emotional perspective, we often explain "benevolence" as "love," hence the term *ren ai* (kind-heartedness or humanity). We know that the Confucian idea of *ren ai* has a peculiar feature, that is, a structured hierarchical love. However, this hierarchical love is often misunderstood, especially by modern humanism, at the expense of ignoring objective existence, which is not easily perceived. For example, here is an understanding of hierarchical love: as I love my parents more than a stranger, the love I give to my parents is significantly different from that I give to a stranger. This explanation shows the hierarchical difference related to the sense of humanity, but it reverses cause and effect. The emotion is not ready-made. If we do not make a deeper analysis but just interpret emotion directly as the reason for ethical behavior, we are bound to fall in the mud of emotionalism.[27] Therefore, we first need to analyze the source and foundation of emotion. In fact, we should focus on hierarchical love according to this. The key to understanding the differences in hierarchical love is that the distance between different degrees of emotion is based on the difference of the objective existence. In other words, there is a difference for love to different people, because the objects we show love for have their objective differences in terms of their existence, i.e., these *are* my parents, that *is* a stranger.[28] It is because of this that the human relationships related to hierarchical love are not only built on objective beings, which constitutes the objective reason for ethical behavior, but are also consistent with the human emotions in our actual life because emotions and objective existence are not going against each other. In a word, in this, regardless of whether man's rationality is working as the objective reason for the ethical behavior or human emotion is working as the subjective motivation for the ethical behavior, this is eventually based on objective being and takes objective being as the principal responsibility. The above-mentioned analysis can show that in Confucianism, the objective reason and the subjective motivation of ethical behavior are consistent. Specifically, the two are unified in the objective being. We can appropriately call it the existential foundation of ethics. Then, can we understand the sense of humanity as a pure sense of moral obligation created by facing the universal moral law? Can we put the Kantian categorical imperative on a par with Confucians' benevolence ethics, which is not only deeply implicated in daily moral human relations and thus with humanity, but also relates to everything in the universe and thus complies with the heavenly principles? It is quite evident that a kind of love that does not follow the proper order does not respect objective being and does not let the principle of benevolence and the emotions of love lay their foundation on objective being. People may say that Kant's deontology is reasonable but not rational, while Confucian ethics is the opposite. This view is still relying on the former position, because the "principle" is the one ignoring objective existence. The inconsistency between reason and emotion here revealed is, in fact, the primary symptom of modern moral philosophy. If objective being is the ultimate foundation, we will see that hierarchical ethical love is a perfectly logical and reasonable ethical idea, while Kantian deontology is neither reasonable nor rational. In other words, if Confucian ethical thought is understood as Kantian deontology, Confucian ethics will also suffer from the "schizophrenia of modern ethical theories," and develop even further a tendency towards moral fanaticism. In fact, this is a serious consequence of Mou Zongsan misappropriating Kant's moral autonomy for the interpretation of Confucian ethics. However, Mou Zongsan is clearly aware of the inconsistency between emotion and reason in Kant's moral philosophy, and this is also a key point for him to criticize in Kant. However, since he fundamentally accepts Kant's deontology, that is to say, he accepts Kant's moral theory disregarding objective existence, therefore, when he stresses the consistency between reason and emotion in Confucianism, he has to take into account the emotion, having the moral reason as his target, so as to make it a means to solve the "schizophrenia" between ethical reason and motivation. Asserting Kantian self-discipline means strengthening the autonomy concept, and further making the subject become a stronger voluntary concept: this is the specific performance for this solution. Because the heavenly principles are converted to moral reasons, human emotion must also be converted to moral emotion. This approach at last results in a loss of both emotion and reason, because the loss of heavenly principles will make it difficult for man's emotion to be preserved.

In addition, Mencius emphasizes the difference between "acting out of *ren yi*" and "putting *ren yi* into practice" which was adopted to prove the consistency between reason and motivation of Confucian ethical behavior, and even used to explain the differences between autonomy and heteronomy. In this regard, there are two interpretations. This Mencian argument appears in the context related to the evaluation of Shun:

> That whereby man differs from the lower animals is but small. The mass of people cast it away, while superior men preserve it. Shun clearly understood the multitude of things and closely observed the relations of humanity. He walked along the path of benevolence and righteousness. He did not need to pursue benevolence and righteousness.
>
> (*Mengzi* IVB.19)

First of all, "walking along the path of benevolence and righteousness" and "pursuing benevolence and righteousness" cannot be regarded as the standard to judge Confucianism. Mencius' first statement ("walking along the path of benevolence and righteousness") here is used to praise the sage Emperor Shun, showing the high level of the path of moral realization. Therefore, the second statement ("pursuing benevolence and righteousness") does not refer to those with the wrong belief but means instead a relatively low level on the path of moral realization. In this regard, Zhu Xi claimed that

> Innate laws of things are used not only to measure the external, and ethics are related to oneself, so the knowledge of them is different in terms of the detail. For Shun, he knew them naturally. He walked along the path of benevolence and righteousness. He did not need to pursue benevolence and righteousness. The benevolence and righteousness had been rooted in the heart. He acted according to it. He didn't act reluctantly just because benevolence and righteousness are virtues but acted only after deep thinking. This is what the sage does, who never fails to preserve it when it needs to be preserved. Yin said: "The one who preserves it is a noble and superior man (*junzi*); who preserves it is a sage. What a noble and superior man preserves is the *tianli* (principle of Heaven); walking along the path of benevolence and righteous is what the preserver can do."

Secondly, one might think that, according to the different levels of moral cultivation, different modes of the relationship between reason and motivation of ethical behavior can be drawn. Only at the sage level can the two be identical. At the lower levels, like the noble level and superior man level, the two are not precisely the same, but there is an obvious tension and even opposition between them. Therefore, asserting that there is a "schizophrenia" between ethical behavior's reason and motivation is somewhat sensational: if so, the noble and superior man will inevitably get "schizophrenia." However, this view is paradoxical. The consistency between reason and motivation derives from the ultimate foundation of objective existence, and that is the root of the "schizophrenia of modern ethical theories." It is because reason-based morality is no longer based on objective being, but the respect and recognition of objective beings are retained in a person's emotion. Thus, the schizophrenia of reason and motivation comes into being. Whether emotion for reason or reason for emotion, they can be seen as a modern solution to this kind of schizophrenia, but they are doomed to fail because they still ignore objective beings. In other words, the schizophrenia between the reason and motivation in ethical behavior does not depend on the existence of some tension between reason and motivation, but depends on what kind of tension there is. If the inconsistency between reason and motivation cannot be overcome in the case that neither is changed, there must be schizophrenia. On the contrary, if the inconsistency between reason and motivation can be overcome so that neither is changed, this inconsistency can only be understood as the manifestation of uncompleted accomplishment on the moral path of cultivation, rather than schizophrenia between reason and motivation.

The above analysis highlights how Confucian ethics can only be classified as virtue ethics rather than deontology.[29] Mou Zongsan's appropriation of the autonomy concept closely related to Judeo-Christian tradition to explain Confucianism consists of replacing the original classical Confucian virtue ethics with law ethics with distinctive modern features, which is, as a result, a modern twist on Confucian ethical thought. However, Mou Zongsan's appropriation is not groundless. We often hear some people say that emphasizing obligation is a significant feature of Confucian ethics. Since Aquinas was able to connect the Christian divine command theory and Aristotle's virtue ethics, we also need to explore further whether there exists or may exist an intellectual form of obligation in traditional Confucian ethics. Or from another point of view, is there a significant possible relationship between an intellectual form and obligation in Confucian ethical tradition?

We have pointed out that obligation is always presented as a command. The following aspects are divided when regarding a command as an event: commander, command behavior, command content and command obedience. For example, speaking of the divine command theory in Judeo-Christian tradition, God is the one who issues the command. The law issued by God is his behavior (i.e., the action performed by who issued the command). So, the content of the law is the content of this command. The man, as who is willing to obey this law, is the one who follows the command, i.e., the follower who shows his obedience to the command. Obligation comes from the behavior performed by the follower, under the premise that someone shall first issue the command. The content of the command is the content of the obligation. When the one who follows the command submits to the command willingly, a sense of duty comes into being. If we speak about the religious ethical tradition of early Confucianism, the "Mandate" is that of Heaven (*tianming*), and it is first associated with an "order" connotation. From an etymological point of view, the Chinese character *ming* ("command") includes *kou* ("mouth") and *ling* ("order"), and is in fact synonymous with *ling* ("order"). And there is some evidence in the Confucian literature. For example, a paragraph in the *Chunqiu Gu Liang Commentary, the First Year of Emperor Zhuang* reports:

> As for Heaven, she has to accept its principle. As for man, she has to accept the order of her husband. If she doesn't obey the heavenly principle, Heaven will abandon her; if she doesn't obey the order of her husband, her husband will abandon her.

Dong Zhongshu quotes the entire sentence in his *Chunqiu Fanlu* (namely *Luxuriant Dew of the Spring and Autumns Annals*). The idea of Heaven issuing his command through words may be the original meaning of "destiny" but it does not occupy a leading position in the formation and spread of Confucianism. What we are familiar with is an opposite view, clearly explained by Confucius: "Does Heaven speak? The four seasons pursue their courses, and all things are continually being produced, but does Heaven say anything?" (*Lunyun* XVII.19). Mencius also believes that Heaven does not "confer its appointment on him (Emperor Shun) with specific injunctions." In answering Wan Zhang, he replies in the same tone: "Heaven does not speak. It simply showed its will by his personal conduct and his conduct of affairs" (*Mengzi* IXB.5). That is to say, the Mandate of Heaven is the most originary and orthodox thinking in Confucianism, but this idea does not mean that Heaven directly issues his commands with words.

So, how does Heaven issue his commands? When it comes to the relationship between Heaven and man, we cannot but discuss the idea of the relation between "virtue" and "human nature." As is well known, in the process of transferring Heaven's Mandate from the Shang dynasty to the Zhou dynasty, the emergence of the idea of "matching Heaven by realizing human virtue" becomes crucial. Heaven bestows some special persons with special gifts which are called "virtue." Virtue means to obtain, to hold on to, to grasp what Heaven bestows. The ones bestowed with virtue undertake a higher heavenly command to protect their people and rule legitimately as king: this means "honoring virtue and protecting the people," and "the truly brilliant is the king, and the king is the father and mother of the people." Therefore, *de*, mentioned above, is not the modern sense of moral "virtue" of morality (*daode*) but refers to the outstanding gift man receives from Heaven. From the quoted texts we can see clearly that intelligence and wisdom are also included in this term *de*, and Heaven blesses those who perform the virtue of Heaven, as "Heaven is impartial and always helps those with virtue." Because "virtue" comes from Heaven, respecting virtue is respecting Heaven, and realizing "virtue" is to follow the Mandate of Heaven, so it can be said "matching Heaven by realizing human virtue." We can see that the emergence of "virtue" contributes to an essential breakthrough in thought about obeying Heaven: Heaven's Mandate is neither abstruse nor ethereal nor showed through definite orders, but bestows someone with virtue to inspire the people. The idea of the virtue of Heaven's Mandate developed into the nature conferred by Heaven. This is quite clearly articulated at the beginning of the *Doctrine of the Mean*: "What Heaven has conferred is called nature." The meaning of "virtue" is the same with that of "nature," so in the *Doctrine of the Mean* we can find the expression *zun dexing* (respect and honor virtue and nature). The difference is that in the context of "matching Heaven by realizing human virtue," maybe only a few people can obtain the excellent "virtue" from Heaven, but in the context of "what Heaven has conferred is called nature," everyone has this innate "nature." This theoretical change is essential to the formation of Confucianism. Confucius' contribution is crucial for this development, while Zisi and Mencius can be seen as the most influential thinkers who carried on this tendency. In understanding and obeying what Heaven commands through "respecting virtue and nature" and adhering to Heaven's Mandate, we can see that Heaven's Mandate becomes a favor bestowed, because virtue and nature are the sources of beauty and kindness. Heaven bestowing man with virtue and nature means that man gets beauty and kindness from Heaven, so obeying what Heaven commands actually means to receive and accept Heaven's favor. Moreover, the evolution from *de* ("virtue") to *xing* ("nature") shows that the favor bestowed by Heaven is not just presented to a few people, but to every man. The emergence of the concept of *dexing* (virtue and nature, as "virtuous integrity") shifts the Confucian concept of Heaven's Mandate towards the idea of virtue ethics, unlike the Judeo-Christian tradition which presents the path of law ethics under a divine command theory.[30]

However, from the above analysis of a command as an "event," we can recognize some traces of the agreement between the concept of command and a specific form of Confucian thought. For example, when we think of idioms like "the emperor sentences me to die, and I must die," "the commands of parents and the words of matchmakers" or "fate cannot be escaped from, and what the husband commands cannot be violated" and others, the importance of the concept of command in ethical life is rather obvious. It is not accidental that these idioms highlight three cardinal principles that have a significant influence in the history of Confucian thought: the ruler who guides the subject, the father who guides the son and the husband who guides the wife. The concept of obligation as the core of Confucianism is associated with these principles. According to the general understanding, the three cardinal principles establish the relationship between command and obedience in the ethical relationship. The ruler is the one who issues the command, and the minister is the one who obeys, and the same relation can be seen for the father and the son, as well as for the husband and the wife. From this, we can recognize two fundamental characteristics: the first illustrates the essence of the three cardinal principles according to the main idea of the concepts of command and obey. If we can assert that the three cardinal principles can constitute Confucian ethics' deontology, obligation derives from command and obedience. The second is that the three cardinal principles establish a unilateral obligation, namely, the obligation of the person who obeys. These two features are familiar to many people in modern times, especially those familiar with the famous criticism of the three cardinal principles proposed by Tan Sitong. However, if analyzed carefully we can see that these three principles, or at least the three cardinal guides interpreted in this way, are rather incompatible with early Confucianism. First of all, regarding the second aspect, a ruling unilateral obligation means that those who issue the command, the ruler, the father and the husband, because they are those who command, have no ethical obligation to those who obey their commands, i.e., the minister, the son and the wife. It is not difficult to see the fallacy of this conclusion. What Confucianism emphasizes is "the ruler shall act as ruler, the minister shall act as minister; the father shall act as a father, and the son shall act as son," which not only presents demands and expectations to the ministers and sons but also puts forward requirements and expectations to the rulers and fathers. In other words, the ruler, the minister, the father and the son have their respective moral paths and principles to be in accord with. If we use the word "obligation" to explain the ethical relationship between the ruler, the minister, the father and the son, obviously, the ruler and father are obliged respectively to the minister and son. The ruler being the ruler is related to the minister. The father being the father is related to the son. The husband being the husband is in relation with the wife. Confucian ethics does not hold the view that the ruler can act not as a ruler but the minister shall act as a minister, or the father can act not as a father but the son must act as a son, or the husband can act not as a husband but the wife must act as a wife. Secondly and more importantly, regarding the first aspect, the concept of command and obedience is not the main idea through which Confucianism understands the ethical relation. Confucius presents a clear reflection on this point:

> The disciple Zeng said, "I have heard your instructions on the affection of love, on respect and reverence, on giving repose to (the minds of) our parents, and on making our names famous. I would venture to ask if (simple) obedience to the orders of one's father can be pronounced filial piety." The Master replied, "What words are these! What words are these! Anciently, if the Son of Heaven had seven ministers who would remonstrate with him, although he had not right methods of government, he would not lose his possession of the kingdom. If the prince of a state had five such ministers, though his measures might be equally wrong, he would not lose his state. If a great officer had three, he would not, in a similar case, lose (the headship of) his clan. If an inferior officer had a friend who would remonstrate with him, a good name would not cease to be connected with his character. And the father who had a son that would remonstrate with him would not sink into the gulf of unrighteous deeds.

Therefore, when a case of unrighteous conduct is concerned, a son must by no means keep from remonstrating with his father, nor a minister from remonstrating with his ruler. Hence, since remonstrance is required in the case of unrighteous conduct, how can (simple) obedience to the orders of a father be accounted filial piety?"

(The Book of Filial Piety)

Similar remarks are recorded in the *Xunzi*:

King Ai of the State of Lu asked the master, "Is the son filial when he obeys the order of his father? Is the minister loyal when he obeys the order of his king?" He repeated the question for three times, but the master didn't reply. The master trotted out and told it to Zi Gong: "A moment ago, the king asked me: 'Is the son filial when he obeys the order of his father? Is the minister loyal when he obeys the order of his king?' He asked it three times and I didn't give him the answer. What's your opinion?" Zi Gong replied: "The son is filial when he obeys the order of his father. The minister is loyal when he obeys the order of his king. Master, what else can you reply?" The master replied: "You are really a child. You don't understand. In the past, if a state with ten thousand chariots had four ministers who would remonstrate with him, it would not have its boundary ceded. If a state with a thousand chariots had three such ministers, the state power wouldn't be in danger; if a scholar-bureaucrat with a hundred chariots had two such ministers, the ancestral temple wouldn't be in doom. If a father had a son who would remonstrate with him, he wouldn't do anything unsuited to the etiquette. If a scholar had a friend who would remonstrate with him, he wouldn't do anything unsuited to moral principles. Therefore, if a son blindly obeys his father, how can he be a filial son? If a minister blindly obeys his king, how can he be a loyal minister? Only when he figures out what he is obeying can he be filial and loyal."

The remonstration discussed here not only exists between the king and his ministers, but also exists between father and son, as well as the scholar and his friend. Confucius stated clearly that the meaning of "the son obeys the order of his father" is not filial piety, and "the minister obeys the order of his king" is not loyalty. The reason is, "only when he figures out what he is obeying can he be filial and loyal." This can explain why Confucian thought did not make order and obedience the purport of understanding the ethical relationship. It has been pointed out above that the Confucian Heaven's Mandate is different from the divine command theory of the Judeo-Christian tradition, and it did not lead to the concept of divine law, so the core concept of its ethics is not obligation closely related to legalism, but virtue. Because of this, even if the concept of Heaven's Mandate is implemented in ethical relations, virtue is still the core to understanding Confucian ethics. Even if in the ancient Chinese social context, we can say that the minister regards the ruler as Heaven, the son sees the father as Heaven and the wife sees the husband as Heaven, this does not mean that the minister, the son and the wife should be absolutely obedient when serving the ruler, the father and the husband.

Therefore, if we take the three cardinal principles as the various propositions that Heaven's Mandate implemented in ethical relations, we can find the source of Confucian deontology. The non-equality in the ethical relationship provides the possibility for command and obedience, but the mere order and obedience cannot be enough to achieve ethical life. Of course, there are obligations in the ethical relationship, but it is not limited to obligations. This point can also be seen from the modern ethical relationship. For example, modern law generally stipulates that parents have an obligation to raise their children, and the children have an obligation to support their parents. However, this does not mean that the ethical relationship between parents and children is limited to the essential obligations stipulated by the law. On the contrary, if there are only the essential obligations of care and support between parents and their children, we will say that this is not only a manifestation of the alienation of affection but also the failure of ethics. Therefore, understanding the ethical relationship as different levels of obligation is the consequence of legalizing ethical relations—in the history of Chinese thought it is the transformation of Confucian ethics through legalism. Perhaps this legalization holds a positive connotation in the sphere of political philosophy, but if it is understood as the essence of ethical relation, it implies a kind of depreciation, particularly when it comes to the ethical relationship which is closely related to self-identity.

In terms of understanding man's ethical life, the concept of responsibility is more important than obligation. Although the two concepts are often confused in Chinese, there are still many differences between the two. An undeniable linguistic fact is that we say "great responsibility" but not "great obligation." It can be seen that responsibility cannot be exerted through specific, precise contents, so there are great and small responsibilities. An obligation as an obligation is always definite, with no difference in degree. Perhaps we can understand obligation as the most basic responsibility, that is, the so-called "minimal," but responsibility exceeds the scope of obligation. The degree of responsibility is often closely related to the ability of the individual who has been assigned responsibility. For example, we always give more responsibility to the élites. However, obligation is always equal and has almost nothing to do with the difference in individual ability. For example, the legal obligation to support parents applies to the rich and the poor, city residents and rural residents.

Clarifying the difference between the two concepts of responsibility and obligation can enable us to better understand our ethical life. Take the ethical relationship between parents and children as an example again. Obviously, we cannot say that a son or daughter who fulfills the legal obligation is a model of filial piety. Children's filial piety towards parents cannot be limited to legal obligations. On the contrary, filial piety understood as a responsibility rather than an obligation knows no limitation. There is no doubt that there is a great difference between basic obligation and great responsibility. Here we refer to the word *xiaodao*, "the path or the principle of filial piety," which is, of course, natural and legitimate. However, it is worth noting that "filial piety" cannot be exactly understood as "the law of filial piety": that is, *dao* here cannot be exactly understood as "law." Obligation is directed at the minimal requirements in the ethical relationship, while responsibility involves the positive orientation in the ethical relationship. The obligation requires that man shall not do this or that, so the performance of the obligation guarantees the lowest level of the essence of what makes man a human being, but responsibility will put forward higher expectations: you can do this or that, meaning you will be a certain kind of person. Obligation regulates what man shall not do and shall not be. Responsibility achieves what a man can do and can be. Since virtue relates to the positive aspect of man's existence and life, in ethical thought focused on virtue, the concept of responsibility is more attuned while the concept of obligation is far from enough. Even though He Lin's effort is to find out the three cardinal principles' peculiar and absolute spiritual nature, he ignores the different approaches to obligation and virtue.[31] On this point, Mou Zongsan is unaware that the difference between obligation and virtue may be related to the tension between Chinese and Western cultures he has inherited, and to the specific resources of Western philosophy he has used.

Notes

1 Alasdair MacIntyre, *After Virtue*, trans. by Song Jijie (Yilin Press, 2003), p. 139.
2 Kant's reason is that we can never infer what we should do from the fact of what God has ordered us to do. In other words, it must be reasonably explained why we should do what God commands. This means that, although Kant does not recognize the Divine Command Theory as equipped with the rationality of morality, what he does not do is completely overthrow the Divine Command Theory, but finds a rational defense through the transformation of the Divine Command Theory, that is, to provide proof of moral rationality. Kant's criticism of the Divine Command Theory can be seen in his *Groundwork of the Metaphysics of Morals*, 4:443, trans. and ed. by Mary J. Gregor (Cambridge University Press, 1996), p. 91. If the "absolutely perfect divine will" is regarded "as the basis of moral system, it is directly opposite to morality." On the same page Kant also stated that, although the moral sense concept and the general sense of the perfect concept (related to God's divine will) cannot lay the foundation for morality, the two will not undermine morality. Therefore, if he must make a choice between the two, he "will choose the latter, because at least it takes the decision of issues away from the sensibility and leads them to a purely rational court."
3 G.W.F. Hegel, "Spirit of Christianity and Its Fate," in *Early Theological Writings*, trans. by He Lin (Commercial Press, 1988), p. 308 (the translation is slightly altered). The title of this section is: "Jesus' Moral Admonition: (a) comparison between the Sermon on the Mount and Mosaic Law and Kantian Ethics." On Hegel's criticism

of Kant's concept of autonomy, see Henry Allison, *Kant's Theory of Freedom*, trans. by Chen Huping (Liaoning Education Press, 2001), p. 276 et seq.

4 Paul Tillich, "Systematic Theology I (Reason and Revelation)," in *Collected Works of Paul Tillich*, Vol. II, trans. by He Guanghu (Shanghai Joint Publishing, 1999), p. 983. On this point, Mou Zongsan categorizes Christian theonomous morality as heteronomous morality, which is not an unbiased view but a rash argument.

5 See Emmanuel Levinas, "Freedom and Command," in *Collected Philosophical Papers*, trans. by Alphonso Lingis (Duquesne University Press, 1987). Nietzsche claimed the heteronomous nature of morality. In his *On the Genealogy of Morals* he said that "'autonomy' and 'morality' are mutually exclusive" (see *On the Genealogy of Morals and Ecco Homo*, trans. by Walter Kaufmann and Reginald J. Hollingdale [Random House, 1967], p. 59). Nietzsche values the concept of autonomy, which he closely relates with the concept of Superman, so autonomy is entirely used by him in the super-moral sense: autonomy corresponds to the master morality rather than the slave morality. It is clear that Max Scheler's concept of personality autonomy is deeply influenced by Nietzsche. On Nietzsche's concept of autonomy, see Keith Ansell-Pearson, "Nietzsche on Autonomy and Morality: the Challenge to Political Theory," *Political Studies*, 1991 (39). On Max Scheler's personality autonomy, see Max Scheler, *The Formalism of Ethics and Material Value Ethics*, trans. by Ni Liangkang (SDX Joint Publishing, 2004), p. 603 et seq.

6 G.E.M. Anscombe, "Modern Moral Philosophy," in Roger Crisp and Michael Slote (eds.), *Virtue Ethics* (Oxford University Press, 1997).

7 See Marcia W. Baron, "Kantian Ethics," in *Three Methods of Ethics: A Debate*. (Blackwell, 1997), p. 34.

8 Immanuel Kant, *Critique of Practical Reason*, 5:30, trans. by Deng Xiaomang, rev. by Yang Zutao (People's Publishing House, 2003), p. 36.

9 Kant, *Groundwork of the Metaphysics of Morals*, 4:422, p. 73.

10 Martin Heidegger holds this view in "A Letter on Humanism," in *Landmark*, trans. by Sun Zhouxing (Commercial Press, 2000). Heidegger straightforwardly claimed that the theme of this article is "reflection on action," and then pointed out that the problem of humanism is the question of "what is man"; in fact, he regards man's being and man's actions as the same thing. Analysis on this point can be found in Jean-Luc Nancy, "Heidegger's 'Originary Ethics,'", in Francois Raffoul and David Pettigrew (eds.), *Heidegger and Practical Philosophy* (State University of New York Press, 2002). In addition, both Kant and Heidegger have a common understanding of the concept of "action," which they consistently trace back to the ancient Greek concept of "practice" (praxis).

11 Martin Heidegger, "Phenomenological Interpretations in Connection with Aristotle: An Indication of the Hermeneutical Situation," in *Supplements: From the Earliest Essays to Being and Time and Beyond*, trans. by John van Buren (State University of New York Press, 2002).

12 Martin Heidegger, *Plato's Sophist*, trans. by Richard Rojcewicz and André Schuwer (Indiana University Press, 1997), p. 33.

13 Bernard Williams, *Ethics and the Limits of Philosophy* (Harvard University Press, 1985), p. 74.

14 Martha Nussbaum puts forward doubt whether Williams' criticism "can leave space for theories like Aristotle." See Martha Nussbaum, "Tragedy and Justice," *Boston Review*, October/November 2003.

15 In fact, Heidegger's criticism of Aristotle's "ethics" in "A Letter on Humanism" is close to the anti-theoretical nature of Williams, and thus he picks out the concept of "originary ethics" to compete with the concept of "ethics" in traditional Western disciplines. Interestingly, this judgment made by Heidegger implies a well-known idea in Aristotle's thought: ethics as a practical science can only correspond to the *phronesis* related to unsettled practical affairs, and cannot correspond to the *sophia* with eternal things as the cognitive object.

16 There is no doubt that historicism is often closely related to nihilism, acting as the life-saving straw of nihilism. On this point, the most representative contribution is the theory of Karl Marx.

17 This can explain why Heidegger greatly appreciates Karl Marx's idea of history, and even this appreciation exceeds his praise for Husserl (see "A Letter on Humanism"). The problem is that, rather than claiming that the foundation of man's being is only built on the flotsam of the past, it would be better to say that man's being loses its foundation. From this we can catch a glimpse of the hidden relation between historicism and nihilism. In addition, although Heidegger basically gives up his frequently applied "truth" at an early stage in *Being and Time*, this concept always played an important role in his thought.

18 Kant, *The Metaphysics of Morals*, 6:394, pp. 524–525.

19 See Wang Rongzu, *Theories of Kang Youwei* (Zhonghua Book Company, 2006), p. 58.

20 Chen Lai, *Ancient Religions and Ethics: The Roots of Confucianism* (SDX Joint Publishing, 1996), p. 301.

21 Matteo Ricci and Nicolas Trigault, *Matteo Ricci's Chinese Commentary*, trans. by He Gaoji, Wang Zunzhong and Li Shenyi (Zhonghua Book Company, 1983), p. 102.

22 Kant, *Groundwork of the Metaphysics of Morals*, 4:400, p. 55.

23 This point will be further discussed in the following chapter.

24 Michael Stocker, "The Schizophrenia of Modern Ethical Theories," in Roger Crisp and Michael Slote (eds.), *Virtue Ethics* (Oxford University Press, 1997), p. 74. Reprinted from *Journal of Philosophy*, 73 (1976), p. 453–466.

25 Bernard Williams, "Persons, Character and Morality," in *Moral Luck* (Cambridge University Press, 1981), p. 18.

26 In the Western tradition related to virtue ethics, virtue is always directly prescribed as a stable disposition through moral cultivation.

27 MacIntyre made a profound analysis and brilliant criticism of the ideological trend to emotionalism in modern Western ethics. See MacIntyre, *After Virtue*.

28 Following Husserl, Heidegger clearly pointed out that the "being" of an object must be understood from the perspective of relationship, that is, 其所是. The understanding of "being" from the perspective of an entity's attribute is derived (even if it is the essential attribute), not to mention the understanding of "being" in modern scientific thinking. In Husserl's words, "essence" is only a formal concept, rather than a universal concept.

29 The difference between virtue ethics and deontology can be interpreted from many perspectives, and I only make a brief analysis of its core. For example, from the contents of virtue ethics, some virtues of the classical virtue ethics are deposed in contemporary deontology and utilitarianism, are no longer part of virtue ethics, but are considered to be non-moral, among which the most famous is wisdom (to be clever and wise). Kant argues the difference between wisdom and morality: he not

only excludes wisdom from the context of morality, he states that they are opposite. For Aristotle, wisdom can be said to be the most important virtue in virtue ethics. In addition, Confucianism and Aristotle represent the two great traditions on virtue ethics in China and the West, and there are profound differences between the two. Since we are focusing on the difference between virtue ethics and deontology, we do not mention the difference between Confucian and Aristotelian ethics. For the differences between the two, see the intellectual dialogue between MacIntyre and Wan Junren, beginning with Alasdair MacIntyre, "Incommensurability, Truth and the Conversation between Confucians and Aristotelians about the Virtues," in E. Deutsch (ed.), *Culture and Modernity* (University of Hawaii Press, 1991). For the Chinese version, see 不可公度性、真理和儒家及亚里士多德主义者关于美德的对话, trans. by Peng Guoxiang, in *Confucian Studies*, 1998 (4.). MacIntyre stresses the differences related to the concept of virtue ethics and ethical thought between Confucianism and Aristotle; hereupon, Wan Junren wrote an article entitled "Contrasting Confucian Virtue Ethics and MacIntyre's Aristotelian Virtue Theory" (儒家美德伦理及其与麦金太尔之亚里士多德主义的视差), in *Chinese Academic*, 2001 (2). The translated English version is by Edward Slingerland, in Robin R. Wang (ed.), *Chinese Philosophy in an Era of Globalization* (State University of New York Press, 2004), which raised some different opinions against MacIntyre. MacIntyre responded to this article with another article, entitled "Once More on Confucian and Aristotelian Conceptions of the Virtues: A Response to Professor Wan," also in Wang, *Chinese Philosophy in an Era of Globalization*; the Chinese version (孔子与亚里士多德的美德概念的再讨论) is translated by Yue Xiukun, in *Chinese Academic*, 2002 (1), , which discussed again some of the main points that both sides introduced.

30 MacIntyre pointed out that Aristotle, as a representative example of virtue ethics, also stressed respect for the law, and he further concluded: "When one presents his life as a whole which realization is performed towards the common beauty and kindness, he must at the same time clarify his ethical life according to virtue and law." See MacIntyre, *After Virtue*, p. 214. In Confucian thought, the corresponding object of law ethics, if any, can only be *li* (courtesy or the ritual etiquette). In this sense, *li* as understood as a virtue by Mencius is quite peculiar: we may draw an analogy with the sense of obligation mentioned by Kant, that is, the respect for obligation. However, it is necessary to point out that in Confucianism, *"li"* can precisely increase and decrease at any time. Therefore, *"li"* closely related to the context of a particular era is fundamentally different from the universal law.

31 In his famous article "New Review on the Five Cardinal Relationships," published on May 1, 1940, in Vol. 3 of *Strategies of the Warring States*, and later collected in *Culture and Life* (Commercial Press, 1988), He Lin made a remarkable interpretation of the absolute ethical knowledge and measurement— what he called "loyalty to ideas"—contained in the three cardinal principles. However, this interpretation still considers the concept of obligation as the core to understanding Confucian ethical thought and makes an analogy between the concept of obligation of Confucian deontology and the Kantian categorical imperative. In addition, the interpretation of the difference between the five cardinal relationships and three cardinal principles from the different standards of absolute and relative is not without problems. In my article "New Review on the Five Cardinal Relationships" I discussed the core points and the limits of this article. See Tang Wenming, *Confucianism in China* (China Social Sciences Press, 2008).

Bibliography

Original Confucian masterpieces and works by Mou Zongsan

Mou Zongsan, *The Wisdom of Life*, San Min Book, 1970.

Mou Zongsan, Features of Chinese Philosophy, Shanghai Ancient Books, 1977.

Mou Zongsan, *Intellectual Intuition and Chinese Philosophy*, Commercial Press (Taiwan), 1980.

Mou Zongsan, *Buddha Nature and Prajna*, Student Book Store, 1984.

Mou Zongsan, *Phenomena and Thing-in-Itself*, Student Book Store, 1984.

Mou Zongsan, *Treatise on the Summum Bonum*, Student Book Store, 1985.

Mou Zongsan, *Moral Idealism*, Student Book Store, 1992.

Mou Zongsan, *The Traits of Chinese Philosophy*, Shanghai Ancient Books, 1997.

Mou Zongsan, The *Substance of Mind and the Substance of Nature*, Shanghai Ancient Books, 1999.

Mou Zongsan, *Collected Works of Mou Zongsan*, 33 vols, Linking Publishing, 2003.

Mou Zongsan, "Geometric Culture and Mathematical Culture," in *Collected Works*, vol. 25.

Mou Zongsan, "Historical Philosophy of Hegel," in *Collected Works*, vol. 17.

Mou Zongsan, "Political Doctrine and Governance Doctrine," in *Collected Works*, vol. 10.

Mou Zongsan, "Records of Cultural Lectures," in *Collected Works*, vol. 28.

Mou Zongsan, "Transcendental Decomposition and Dialectical Comprehensiveness," *Collected Works*, vol. 27.

Mou Zongsan, *Nature, Talent and Metaphysical Reason*, Guangxi Normal University Press, 2006.

Mou Zongsan, *Historical Philosophy*, Guangxi Normal University Press, 2007.

Works by Kant and Hegel

Immanuel Kant, *Groundwork of the Metaphysics of Morals*, trans. by Tang Yue, Commercial Press, 1959.

Immanuel Kant, Critique of Practical Reason, trans. by Guan Wenyun, Commercial Press, 1960.

Immanuel Kant, *Kant's Moral Philosophy*, trans. and annotated by Mou Zongsan, Student Book Store, 1983.

Immanuel Kant, Critique of Judgement, trans. by Werner Pluhar, Hackett, 1987.

Immanuel Kant, *Groundwork of the Metaphysics of Morals*, trans. by Miao Litian, Shanghai People's Publishing House, 1986.

Immanuel Kant, *Critique of Pure Reason*, trans. by Mou Zongsan, Student Book Store, 1992.

Immanuel Kant, *Critique of Judgement*, trans. and annotated by Mou Zongsan, Student Book Store, 1993.

Immanuel Kant, *Practical Philosophy*, trans. and ed. by Mary. J. Gregor, Cambridge University Press, 1996.

Immanuel Kant, *Critique of Pure Reason*, trans. by Paul Guyer and Allen W. Wood, Cambridge University Press, 1998.

Immanuel Kant, *Critique of Practical Reason*, trans. by Han Shuifa, Commercial Press, 1999.

Immanuel Kant, *Critique of the Power of Judgement*, trans. by Paul Guyer and Eric Matthews, Cambridge University Press, 2000.

Immanuel Kant, *Critique of Judegment*, trans. by Deng Xiaomang, ed. by Yang Zutao, People's Publishing House, 2002.

Immanuel Kant, *Critique of Practical Reason*, trans. by Deng Xiaomang, rev. by Yang Zutao, People's Publishing House, 2003.

Immanuel Kant, *Metaphysical Foundations of Natural Science*, trans. by Deng Xiaomang, Shanghai People's Publishing House, 2003.

Immanuel Kant, *Critique of Pure Reason*, trans. by Deng Xiaomang, ed. by Yang Zutao, People's Publishing House, 2004.

Immanuel Kant, "Moral Metaphysics," trans. by Zhang Rong and Li Qiuling, in *Kant's Works*, vol. 6, ed. by Li Qiuling, China Renmin University Press, 2007.

Immanuel Kant, "Religion within the Bounds of Pure Reason," trans. by Zhang Rong and Li Qiuling, in *Kant's Works*, vol. 6.

G.W.F. Hegel, *Hegel's Philosophy of Mind*, trans. from The Encyclopedia of the Philosophical Sciences, trans. by William Wallace, Clarendon Press, 1892.

G.W.F. Hegel, *The Logic of Hegel*, trans. by He Ling, SDX Joint Publishing, 1954.

G.W.F. Hegel, *The Philosophy of History*, trans. by J. Sibree, Dover, 1956.

G.W.F. Hegel, *The Philosophy of Right*, trans. by Fan Yang and Zhang Qitai, Commercial Press, 1961.

G.W.F. Hegel, *Hegel s Philosophy of Right*, trans. T.M. Knox, Oxford University Press, 1967.

G.W.F. Hegel, *Lectures on the Philosophy of World History*, trans. by H.B. Nisbet, Cambridge University Press, 1975.

G.W.F. Hegel, *Hegel's Early Theological Writings*, trans. by He Ling, Commercial Press, 1988.

G.W.F. Hegel, *Philosophy of History*, trans. by Wang Zaoshi, Shanghai Bookstore, 1999.

Other works in Chinese

Henry Allison, *Kant's Theory of Freedom*, trans. by Chen Huping, Liaoning Education, 2001.

Ba Xinsheng, Research on Ethics of the Western Zhou Dynasty, Tianjin Classics, 1997.

Cai Renhou, *Chronicle of Mou Zongsan's Study and Thoughts*, Student Book Store, 1996.

Chen Lai, *Ancient Religions and Ethics:* The Roots of Confucianism, SDX Joint Publishing, 1996.

Chen Lai, "The Problem of Mysticism in the Tradition of the Studies of Mind," in *Realm of Having or Not: Spirit of Wang Yangming's Philosophy*, People's Publishing House, 1991.

Chen Lai, "Mysticism in Feng Youlan's Philosophy," in *Track for Modern Chinese Philosophy*, People's Publishing House, 2001.

Chen Mengjia, Survey of Yin Ruins Oracle Inscriptions, Zhonghua Book Company, 1988.

Cheng Hao and Cheng Yi, *Collected Works of Cheng Yi and Cheng Hao*, ed. by Wang Xiaoyu, Zhonghua Book Company, 2004.

Paul Delicy, *Collected Works of Delicy*, ed. by He Guanghu, Shanghai Joint Publishing, 1999.

Deng Xiaomang, "Three Modules of Possible Golden Rules in Global Ethics," *Jiangsu Social Sciences*, 2002 (4), pp. 1–6.

Deng Xiaomang, *Several Issues of Kant's Philosophy*, SDX Joint Publishing, 2006.

Du Weiming, *Collected Works of Du Weiming*, Wuhan, 2002.

Duan Yucai, *Etymological Dictionary of Characters with Notes*, Shanghai Ancient Books, 1988.

Michel Foucault, "Nietzsche, Genealogy, History", trans. by Su Li, in Liu Xiaofeng and Ni Weiguo (eds.), *Nietzsche in the West*, Shanghai Joint Publishing, 2002, pp. 279–305.

Hans-Georg Gadamer, *Truth and Method*, trans. by Gong Handing, Shanghai Translation, 1999.

He Lin, *Culture and Life*, Commercial Press, 1988.

Martin Heidegger, *Selected Works of Martin Heidegger*, ed. by Sun Zhouxing, Shanghai Joint Publishing, 1996.

Martin Heidegger, *Being and Time*, trans. by Chen Jiaying and Wang Qingjie, ed. by Chen Jiaying, SDX Joint Publishing, 1999.

Martin Heidegger, "A Letter on Humanism," in *Landmark*, trans. by Sun Zhouxing, Commercial Press, 2000, pp. 366–429.

Hou Wailu, *General History of Chinese Thought*, vol. 1, People's Publishing House, 1957.

Huang Zongxi and Quan Zuwang, *Cases in Song and Yuan Dynasties*, Zhonghua Book Company, 1986.

Edmund Husserl, *Ideas: General Introduction to Pure Phenomenology*, trans. by Li Youzheng, Commercial Press, 1992.

Jiang Nianfeng, "Taiwan's Experience after War and Hegel in the Thought of Kang Junyi and Mou Zongsan," in *Text and Practice*, Guiguan Book, 2000.

Lai Gongou, "Core of Cultural Life of Mou Zongsan's Historical Philosophy," *Jiangxi Social Sciences*, 2003 (11), pp. 29–33.

Li Hanji, "Mou Zongsan's Political Idea and Introspection on Hegel's Historical Philosophy," in *Contemporary Confucianism and Western Culture: Philosophy*, Institute of Chinese Literature and Philosophy of Academia Sinica, 2004.

Li Minghui, "On the So-called 'Confucianism Extensive Moralism,'" in *Confucianism and Modern Sense*, Wenjin, 1911.

Li Minghui, *Confucianism and Kant*, Linking Publishing, 1990.

Li Minghui, "Contemporary Neo-Confucianism Orthodoxy," in *Self-transformation of Contemporary Confucianism*, Institute of Chinese Literature and Philosophy of Academia Sinica, 1994.

Li Rongtian, "New Path of Confucianism from Hegel's Historical Philosophy," in *Memoir of the First International Academic Conference of Contemporary Confucianism*, 1991.

Li Zehou, *Five Sayings on Yi Mao*, SDX Joint Publishing, 2003.

Liang Shuming, *The Substance of Chinese Culture*, Xuelin Publishing House, 1987.

Liang Tao, "Symposium on Guodian Inscribed bamboo-slips & School of Zisi-Menciu", Studies on Chinese Intellectual History, 2005 (4).

Lin Huowang, On Knowledge and Behavior from Confucian Concern-Consciousness, Zhengzhong Book Company, 1981.

Liu Yizheng, *Essence of the History of China*, Zhonghua Book Company, 1948.

Luo Yijun, "The Third Phrase Confucius Conception of Mou Zongsan and the Doctrine of Pay Equal Attention to Three Orthodoxies," *Yantai University Journal*, 2005 (2).

Alasdair MacIntyre, *After Virtue*, trans. by Song Jijie, Yilin Press, 2003.

Memoir Editor Group of Mou Zongsan's 70th Birthday Celebration, *Philosophy and Masterpieces of Mou Zongsan*, Student Book Store, 1978.

Ni Liangkang, "Basic Implication of Kant's Intellektuelle Anschauung Concept," *Philosophy Research*, 2001 (10).

Pei Xuehai, Collective Explanations on Empty Words of Ancient Texts, Zhonghua Book Company, 2004.

Qian Mu, *Outline History*, National Translation and Compilation Center, 1956.

Qiu Huanghai, "The Critical Demonstration of Mr. Mou Zongsan's Conception of History," *E'Hu Magazine*, 1999 (5).

Matteo Ricci and Nicolas Trigault, *De Christiana expeditione apud sinas* [*Matteo Ricci's Chinese Commentary*], trans. by He Gaoji, Wang Zunzhong and Li Shenyi, Zhonghua Book Company, 1983.

Jean-Jaques Rousseau, *The Social Contract*, trans. by He Zhaowu, Commercial Press, 1980.

Bertrand Russell, *A History of Western Philosophy*, trans. by Ma Yuande, Commercial Press, 1976.

Max Scheler, *Scheler Anthology*, ed. by Liu Xiaofeng, Shanghai Joint Publishing, 1999.

Max Scheler, The Formalism of Ethics and Material Value Ethics, trans. by Ni Liangkang, SDX Joint Publishing, 2004.

Sun Yatsen, "The Three People's Principles," in *Sun Yatsen Anthology*, People's Publishing House, 1981.

Tang Junyi, On the Origin of Chinese Philosophy: Introduction, Xinya Academy Research Institute, 1974.

Tang Junyi, "The Philosophical Interception of Chinese History," Appendix 1 of *Historical Philosophy*, Guangxi Normal University Press, 2001.

Tang Wenming, *With Life, with Kernel: The Spirit and Modernity Problem of the Original Confucian Ethics*, Hebei University Press, 2002.

Tang Wenming, *Recent Worry: Culture Politics and the Future of China*, East China Normal University Press, 2010.

Charles Taylor, *Hegel and Modern Society*, trans. by Xu Wenrui, Linking Publishing, 1990.

Paul Tillich, "Systematic Theology I (Reason and Revelation)," in Collected Works of Paul Tillich, vol. 2, trans. by He Guanghu, Shanghai Joint Publishing, 1999.

Wan Junren, "Contrasting Confucian Virtue Ethics and MacIntyre's Aristotelian Virture Theory," *Chinese Academic*, 2001 (2).

Wang Bo, "Early Confucianism's Theory on Ren and Yi," *Peking University Journal of Philosophy*, 2005 (11).

Wang Depei, "Book Reading Notes of Truth Seeking (I)," *Journal of Tianjin Normal University*, 1983 (4).

Wang Depei, "Notes on Liji, vol. 1," *Journal of Tianjin Normal University*, 1997 (4).

Wang Guowei, Collected Essays of Wang Guowei, Zhonghua Book Company, 1959.

Wang Guowei, *Posthumous Papers of Wang Guowei*, Shanghai Ancient Books, 1983.

Wang Rongzu, *Theories of Kang Youwei*, Zhonghua Book Company, 2006.

Wang Shenxing, "On the Essence of the Western Zhou Dynasty's Filial Values," *Journal of Humanities*, 1991 (2).

Xu Fuguan, History of Human Nature in China: The Pre-Qin Period, Shanghai Joint Publishing, 2001.

Zhang Xianglong, Martin *Heidegger' Biography*, Hebei People's Press, 1998.

Zhang Zai, *Collected Works of Zhang Zai*, Zhonghua Book Company, 1978.

Zheng Kai, Between Virtue and Propriety: The History of Thought of the Pre-Qin Period, SDX Joint Publishing, 2009.

Zhu Bokun, "Concern-Consciousness and the Ethnic Spirit of the Book of Changes," *Journal of Peking University*, 1997 (1).

Zhu Xi, *The Collected Four Books*, Zhonghua Book Company, 2012.

Other works in English

G.E.M. Anscombe, "Modern Moral Philosophy," in Roger Crisp and Michael Slote (eds.), *Virtue Ethics*, Oxford University Press, 1997.

Keith Ansell-Pearson, "Nietzsche on Autonomy and Morality: The Challenge to Political Theory," *Political Studies*, 1991 (39).

Marcia W. Baron,"Kantian Ethics," in *Three Methods of Ethics: A Debate*, Blackwell, 1997.

Peter K. Bol, *Neo-Confucianism in History*, Harvard University Press, 2008.

Hans-Georg Gadamer, *Truth and Method*, trans. by Joel Weinsheimer and Donald G. Marshall, 2nd rev. edn, Continuum, 2004.

Martin Heidegger, *Kant and the Problem of Metaphysics*, trans. by Richard Taft, Indiana University Press, 1990.

Martin Heidegger, *Plato's Sophist*, trans. by Richard Rojcewicz and André Schuwer, Indiana University Press, 1997.

Martin Heidegger, *The Essence of Human Freedom: An Introduction to Philosophy*, trans. by Ted Sadler, Continuum, 2002.

Martin Heidegger, "Phenomenological Interpretations in Connection with Aristotle: An Indication of the Hermeneutical Situation," in *Supplements: From the Earliest Essays to Being and Time and Beyond*, trans. by John van Buren, State University of New York Press, 2002.

Kenneth Holloway, *Guodian: The Newly Discovered Seeds of Chinese Religious and Political Philosophy*, Oxford University Press, 2009.

P.J. Ivanhoe and B.W. Van Norden (eds.), *Readings in Classical Chinese Philosophy*, Hackett Publishing, 2005.

Ian Johnston (trans.), *The Mozi: A Complete Translation*, Columbia University Press, 2010.

T.M. Knox, "Preface for English Version of Hegel's *Philosophy of Right*", in *Hegel's Philosophy of Right*, trans. by T.M. Knox, Oxford University Press, 1967.

James Legge (trans.), *The Chinese Classics: With a Translation, Critical and Exegetical Notes, Prolegomena, and Copious Indexes. Confucian Analects, the Great Learning, and the Doctrine of the Mean*, 5 vols., Trübner, 1861–1872.

Emmanuel Levinas, "Freedom and Command," in *Collected Philosophical Papers*, trans. by Alphonso Lingis, Duquesne University Press, 1987.

Alasdair MacIntyre, "Incommensurability, Truth and the Conversation between Confucians and Aristotelians about the Virtues," in E. Deutsch (ed.), *Culture and Modernity*, University of Hawaii Press, 1991.

Alasdair MacIntyre, "Once More on Confucian and Aristotelian Conceptions of the Virtues: A Response to Professor Wan," in Robin R. Wang (ed.), *Chinese Philosophy in an Era of Globalization*, State University of New York Press, 2004.

Jean-Luc Nancy, "Heidegger's 'Originary Ethics,'" in Francois Raffoul and David Pettigrew (eds.), *Heidegger and Practical Philosophy*, State University of New York Press, 2002.

Friedrich Nietzsche, *On the Genealogy of Morals and Ecce Homo*, trans. by Walter Kaufmann and Reginald J. Hollingdale, Random House, 1967.

Friedrich Nietzsche, *The Gay Science*, trans. by Walter Kaufmann, Random House, 1974.

Martha Nussbaum, "Tragedy and Justice," *Boston Review*, October/November 2003.

Jean-Jacques Rousseau, *The Social Contract and the First and Second Discourses*, ed. by Susan Dunn, Yale University Press, 2002.

J.B. Schneewind, *The Invention of Autonomy: A History of Modern Moral Philosophy*, Cambridge University Press, 1997.

Michael Stocker, "The Schizophrenia of Modem Ethical Theories", in Roger Crisp and Michael Slote (eds.), *Virtue Ethics*, Oxford University Press, 1997.

Wan Junren, "Contrasting Confucian Virtue Ethics and MacIntyre's Aristotelian Virture Theory," trans. by Edward Slingerland, in Robin R. Wang (ed.), *Chinese Philosophy in an Era of Globalization*, State University of New York Press, 2004.

Bernard Williams, *Moral Luck*, Cambridge University Press, 1981.

Bernard Williams, *Ethics and the Limits of Philosophy*, Harvard University Press, 1985.

Bernard Williams, *Shame and Necessity*, University of California Press, 1993.

Susan Wolf, "Moral Saints," *Journal of Philosophy*, 1982 (8).

Allen W. Wood, *Kant's Ethical Thought*, Cambridge University Press, 1999.

Index